BACK TO THE BEGINNING

To Joyce,
with Love,
Kristen
8/8/19.

Back
To The Beginning

The Progress of a Pilgrim Healer

by

Kirsten Bolwig

A W A Y
Publications
2011

First published by Away Publications, Bath 2011

Cover design and illustrations © Kirsten Bolwig

A catalogue record for this book is available from
the British Library.

Design and book production by Ben Please
www.benedictplease.co.uk

ISBN 978–0–9530330–9-6

Printed in England

This book is dedicated to my son Kieran Sheehy,
my sister Janet Kirk, and Peter Please without whom
this book would not have been completed.

*

With grateful thanks to Palden Jenkins,
Helen and David Hamblin, Gloria Goodsell
and Vivien Womersley for their keen and
critical eyes and helpful remarks.

CONTENTS

PICKING UP THE TRAIL

A FORK IN THE ROAD

PICKING UP THE TRAIL

HEALER HEAL THYSELF

'The goal of a hero's journey is yourself, finding yourself.'
Joseph Campbell
'We are the hero of our own journey.'
Mary McCarthy

From the beginning there was some confusion about my identity. As she departed the maternity hospital, my mother looked down at the baby she was holding and remarked, 'She is much prettier than I thought. She was a funny little thing the last time I held her.' Whereupon the nurse looked at the wristband, whisked away *Baby Rosenberg* and placed me in my mother's arms a moment later. This unfortunate start must have left a psychic imprint for I seem to have spent a large part of my life trying to establish who I am.

I do not consider myself a weird person yet I admit few people have had the strange experience in childhood of watching a lampshade unscrew itself during a burst of telekinesis triggered by a temper tantrum. In fact few people believe anything like this happens other than in the imagination of screenwriters.

Strange experiences are scattered throughout my life, moments that were significant factors in dictating the steps

I have made as a healer. Such as feeling powerful energy flow through me, watching it pour out of my hands as blue-white streams of light, which pulsed and shimmered round my fingertips; hot energy that radiated from my palms like heat waves off tarmac. Or the time I found a stone finger pointing to an ancient artefact buried in the mud of the Severn Estuary.

What does it mean to be psychically gifted and a healer? Where did it all start? It has taken all my life to address these questions and sometimes I feel I have journeyed far only to arrive back at the beginning.

For every healer there comes a time when they have to acknowledge they have a gift. With me, the beginning of this conscious acceptance happened in an ordinary English suburb while holding the arthritic hand of a little old lady who lived a few doors farther down the road. The hand that toasted me with a glass of sherry a week later was definitely less deformed. Other moments followed, some directly connected to healing, some not. All contributed to the unfolding realization that I had a way with healing.

Having lived beyond sixty, I have been overtaken by the desire to write down my experiences as a way of discovering not only where I have come from but also where I am going. Like a tracker, I have had to retrace the route I chose, examining the significant moments I call my footsteps. The task has been a bit like doing a jigsaw puzzle and trying to find where the pieces fit in, seeing the events of my life afresh. Some pieces connect easily together bringing what was a meaningless blur sharply into focus. Others fit only with difficulty defying any simplistic understanding. Some pieces are still missing from the picture. They tantalize me. I know and I don't know.

My origins are composed of two completely different strands, African and Western, and both have influenced my development as a healer. Africa - the cradle of mankind, the land of my birth though not my lineage - has fed me the gift of nature's energy and uncompromising beauty and the rootedness of ancient rhythms. Europe is the mind of Western mysticism and metaphysical insights. Both sides co-exist within me and demand expression. Both are equally important.

To begin, I must return to Africa - to my childhood – and trace the footprints that are scattered there. There is a cellular longing in me that still calls Africa 'home' notwithstanding the fact that all my adult life has been lived in the West. Anthropologists, who in the past looked at societies as far removed from Western culture as possible, are now beginning to turn the lens back on our own society, recognizing that our way of life is at odds with the needs of the world. The pulse of the ancient continent is beginning to call to my aboriginal self with an insistent message for re-alignment, of once more stepping in rhythm with nature.

My life could be likened to a mythical journey encapsulating a search for meaning and purpose for that which is hidden. The drive in me is to move forward in the knowledge that there is something just out of sight, waiting to be found.

This book of footsteps charts the significant moments that have moulded the course of my life, developing the perceptions and insights that have led me to where I am today. There are two threads: the progress of the pilgrim and the progress of the healer. Sometimes the book is about the pilgrim, sometimes about the healer. Sometimes about both. It is as much about the pilgrim as about the healer.

Much has been left out in order to maintain flow in the narrative. I have included difficulties and discoveries, challenges and absurdities, the mystical and profound, and the everyday dimensions when they are telling. Perhaps in the end I will find there are more questions than answers.

SOUTH AFRICAN CHILDHOOD

'Life can only be understood backwards but it must be lived forwards.'
Niels Bohr

In the sunny corner of a room I have created a small altar carefully decorated with significant items: a nightlight in a holder shaped like a sunflower, a Neolithic axe, a stone spiral, a collection of coloured crystals sparkling with rainbows, an owl's feather. My eye is caught by a piece of snakeskin. Once a focus of fear, snakes now represent transformation and renewal for me. The skin is a faded memento of my childhood, a reminder of the python – poor thing – killed at the bottom of the garden by a frightened visitor.

Being observant is a significant aspect of the healing temperament. I trace back through my life, hunting for clues to support this assertion and find them without difficulty in my early South African childhood. As a little bush girl with the freedom to roam, I quickly learned that I had to be unusually observant if I wished to survive. Even after all these years the skill remains.

It was born out recently when I got a speeding ticket and attended a 'safe-motoring' workshop. Following a short video, we were asked what we had seen. It turned out that

I was the only person who had noticed distant detail first, then worked my way towards the foreground. I think this stems from my childhood where I learnt early on that it is wise to look ahead when walking through African bush. It is a necessary survival strategy in a country full of snakes, where puff adders, blending with the surroundings, sunned themselves awake in clearings, where ringhals and the odd mamba found it convenient to use the same path as oneself, where the unwary traveller might get tangled with a boomslang hanging down from a branch overhead.

The memories return as stories:

As an eight-year-old, I was intoxicated with adventure. Seeing myself as an intrepid explorer moulded from the same stuff as Colonel Fawcett of the Amazon, I decided to raid the overgrown gardens of an abandoned house not far from where I lived in Windsor Woods, a eucalyptus plantation situated on the outskirts of Johannesburg. To reach this house I had to follow a path through these shaggy-barked giants standing straight and proud until I arrived at a crossroad of dirt avenues. I snuffed the pungent scents released into the warm air by the different eucalypts; the sweet light scent of a soft round-leafed bush contrasted with the strong aggressive smell of volatile oils released by narrow leafed varieties.

At the crossroads I emerged from deep shade into bright sunshine and eagerly plunged into the tangled growth of the deserted garden opposite, hoping to find almonds ripe for the picking in their soft velvet overcoats. I struggled through the Amazon jungle of my fertile imagination, hacking at grape vines that became strangling lianas.

Once satisfied with my explorations, I returned to the crossroads but stopped abruptly when I stepped into the shade of the eucalypts. My eyes, always scanning ahead, spotted something that hadn't been there before. Something that moved. In the dimmed light, I saw the rearing form of a large, grey ringhals, the South African spitting cobra. With hood spread wide on either side of its blunt head, it fixed gleaming eyes on me, its tongue flickering lightening fast through the diamond-

shape opening at the tip. The jaws were closed, the fangs tucked out of sight but spring-loaded for action if I behaved aggressively. Only my unconscious habit of studying everything in front of me had prevented me from walking straight into it and being bitten or blinded by its venom.

I halted out of range. The snake's tongue flickered again to pick up my scent. Tasting me. Was I a threat? We regarded each other, letting our mutual shock subside. Slowly the ringhals collapsed its hood, lowered its head to slither away through the trees, its scales rasping softly on fallen leaves. The sinuous grey form retreated as a whispering sound. I became conscious that I was holding my breath and that my oxygen-starved lungs were beginning to hurt. Taking a deep breath and with eyes still fixed on the retreating snake, I cautiously walked in a wide arc until I reached the path and ran for home.

I was a child of the bush. A great deal of my time was spent playing alone and as a consequence I developed a richly creative imaginary life. I imagined shrinking to *Borrower* size (the tiny people of Mary Norton's fantasy novels) and going on great expeditions, an explorer of the rockery

undergrowth. Small, lead farm animals, purloined from my sister, became the expeditionary force I was leading. Horses and cows and brawny labourers, frozen in their activity on green metal stands, were marched up and down the steep terraces. I experienced the bravery of scaling the sheer cliff faces of the various rockery stones, traversing the dangerous ledges and hacking my way through the jungle of the flowerbeds. Outside the garden boundaries, dongas (gullies carved out by rain) became ravines in my imagination; the tree roots, great obstacles to get around.

This fantasy world expanded my awareness of the vastness of existence. I would pause, crouched in my play, watching insects and feel in contact with something much greater than myself. There were moments when I felt part of everything. Yet at other times I felt hopelessly lost, a tiny spot in the vast world of my own creation. Being lost developed my sense of adventure and the instinct to explore. It translated into long rambles through the eucalyptus wood and wading through the waist-high grass of the high veldt beyond it, or scrambling to the top of a small kopje (hill) close by. There was much to occupy a young tomboy.

The surroundings contained a feast of sights and sounds. Exquisite weaverbird nests hung, like pendulous fruit, from the branches of eucalyptus trees. The air above me throbbed with the sound of wings in flight. Handsome male birds, in yellow and black plumage, expertly wove basket nests while the small dowdy females sat on nearby branches waiting to inspect the elaborate creations by invitation. The trees heaved and shivered with shrill sounds of noisy competition as the males worked to complete their nests. It was a sound-weave every bit as intricate as the beautiful baskets on display.

After watching this drama unfolding above my head, I would wander off in search of bits to remove from rusting cars lying abandoned on the veldt beyond the trees. I would go home dragging radiators, steering wheels, spark plugs, dials and brake-levers – anything movable. The scavenged booty found its way into adventures my sister and I created amongst the fallen branches of a giant eucalyptus tree. Its trunk metamorphosed from an expeditionary ship one minute to a pirate ship the next. I was always the engineer and mechanic with my bits of engine wedged amongst the branches in the 'boiler room'. The engine 'broke down' frequently, allowing me hours of happy tinkering, like a young Charlie Allnut, while my captain-sister stretched out on the 'deck' above scanning the ocean-veldt for danger with my father's borrowed binoculars. The film *The African Queen* has always been a favourite of mine because of its echoes with those early games we played.

I was not afraid of being alone. The skills I developed playing in the African bush – observation, imagination, heightened awareness and sensitivity – are today essential elements of my healing. Useful now maybe, but as a child I struggled with both sensitivity and a strong, wilful ego.

As an argumentative child I went through a difficult period when I started school. I was filled with questions and adults did not appreciate this. Asking who decided that one and one made two resulted in me being sent out of class within a few weeks of starting. I hated being told that I talked nonsense. On one occasion, I contradicted a professor who said peanuts grew on bushes. I was forced to apologize but knew that they grew underground. It was all very bewildering. I felt a desperate need to be believed but arguing with adults got me into trouble, as this story illustrates.

One mealtime I was sent out for arguing and told to stay in the entrance hall. I slammed the living room door as I left and stood with my back to my mother's black writing desk in the corner. A corkscrew of wound up fury tightened every muscle in my trembling body. It wasn't fair, I thought, and banged my backside hard against the desk making it rock. It made a satisfyingly loud noise. Good! I repeated it again and again, feeling vindictive, gleeful about the noise I was making, knowing it would thoroughly irritate my family and spoil their lunch. I knew it would result in a spanking but I did not care. The door was flung open and my father appeared, but instead of the expected anger, his face turned ashen. I froze, not understanding what was happening. At that moment, Letty, our house servant, appeared through the kitchen door opposite. She dropped the tray with a wild shriek, turned tail and fled. Fear rooted me to the spot and that probably saved my life.

My father spoke quietly in a clear, slow voice. 'Kirsten, when I count to three I want you to jump as far as you can. Try and reach the kitchen

door. Then I want you to run as fast as you can after Letty. One, two, three, JUMP!'

I jumped and ran without looking back, I was so frightened. Letty was outside, her face an ugly, pasty brown. She hugged me fiercely against her soft, ample bosom. 'Oh Koesie! I thought you would die! There's a big snake under the desk. A big, big snake.'

A ringhals, the South African spitting cobra, had found its way into the hall through the open stable door and had curled up in the dark until I had disturbed it by rocking the desk. Letty and my father, entering through their respective doorways, had both seen the snake swaying between my legs, its hood extended revealing the white band from which it gets its name, an embodiment of cold menace ready to strike.

As I struggled free of Letty's embrace, my father appeared in full bee-keeping outfit and wellington boots. On his head he wore a pith helmet complete with fine gauze netting to protect his face and eyes; his hands and arms were encased in the thick hide gloves he used to protect himself when handling baboons.

Armed with a knobkerrie, the Zulu fighting stick, he locked himself inside the entrance hall with the snake. In safety, we listened to the stick thudding against the walls and floor and the answering hiss of the snake accompanying a sound like the squirt of a water gun striking the door. I listened, awed, my fear forgotten. Suddenly I saw my father - my studious, seriously academic father - as a hero! There he was facing a deadly enemy, alone, fighting for his family. How brave he was! Suddenly I was glad he was my father and not one of those handsome, blond, sporty, South African fathers I had often longed for.

Eventually the stick fell silent and the door opened. Behind my father the walls dripped with venom, the floor slippery with the frothy liquid. Lying limply against the wall on the far side was the biggest ringhals I had ever seen. Dad eased the snake onto the end of the knobkerrie. There it hung limply, sadly pathetic, the hood proud no longer, just two loose flaps of skin behind the bloodied head. I was filled with curiosity.

With a pair of forceps he took from his pocket, my father prized open the broken jaws and gently eased the reptile's fangs into view, two large and wickedly curved needles. Unable to suppress the educator in himself, he palpated the venom sac to demonstrate how the poison flowed through the hollow fangs. A large drop of clear yellow liquid appeared at the tip of each fang.

My mother and sister joined me to gaze in wonder. Dad showed us the site of its genitals. It was a male snake. 'Don't you think he is a handsome fellow?' he enthused. We watched the scalpel blade in his steady hand slicing through the skin revealing the muscles and bones that lay beneath, dissecting the heart, lungs and digestive system, as he explained how everything worked. He showed us how the scales helped the snake to move.

Our curiosity bubbled over in questions as the poor snake, relinquishing the last shred of dignity, lost its skin beneath the swift strokes of the scalpel. There it lay, baby pink and pathetic on the study table.

Letty could be heard in the kitchen banging pots and pans. She was still upset. Nothing would induce her to approach the snake. She did not approve of her beloved girls being encouraged to approach this poisonous creature, dead though it was. Snakes were snakes. They were all dangerous as far as she was concerned, with or without their skin.

Animals were central to my childhood and being surrounded by them had a subtle impact on my future as a healer. My father, a zoologist, had a consuming interest in animal-behaviour. Meerkats and ground squirrels arrived shortly after my father's trip to the Kalahari Desert to learn about desert creatures and their habits from Bushmen, an ancient race of people living on the edges of survival. From them he also learnt desert survival skills. Laurens van der Post followed in my father's footsteps a few years later, aided by his experiences and advice.

But it was primates in particular that absorbed my father's interest. Through them he could study individual and group behaviour. Before long we had a large enclosure erected for some vervet monkeys, and an enormously strong, very large cage complete with tree trunks and rubber tyres swings to house a pair of young chacma baboons. The family became used to seeing my father inside the cage, quietly observing them and making copious notes. Later at the dinner table we listened as he shared what he had learned about their behaviour. Without knowing it, I developed a capacity of my own for behavioural understanding.

Over the years, my father's interest progressed to include comparative studies in infant development of primates and humans. More and more books on child psychology and infant rearing appeared on the bookshelves.

Then in 1959, when South Africa became a republic and Apartheid became fully established, the family moved from South Africa to Uganda and there, Freddy, a baby patas monkey, joined our family. Suddenly, research into infant development became part of family life and I found a replacement for the dolls that had been left behind in South Africa.

Even with his tail stretched out, Freddy would not have measured the length of a biro pen when he came into our care. He was a minute and fragile, five-day-old patas monkey who had been dropped by his mother as she escaped from the mealie (sweet corn) fields of an irate African farmer. Like all infants he needed constant care and regular feeding - and lots of loving attention. I enjoyed the ritual of putting him down to sleep wrapped in a version of swaddling clothes to make him feel secure. Freddy, squawking shrilly like a little bird, was placed on one edge and quickly rolled up, leaving just his small, black, wrinkled face poking out at one end.

On maternity duty I would rock him to sleep, crooning soft nonsense words to him as I watched his tiny pink eyelids grow heavy and finally shut. In sleep all the worry lines inherited from his ancient genetic past slowly erased from his tiny face. Peace and harmony had been restored. Something deep within my child's psyche was satisfied.

As he grew, Freddy became inseparable from my father, riding on his shoulder into the lecture halls. He resisted the blanket, clinging instead to my father for security; arms wrapped tightly round an ankle, out of sight inside a baggy trouser leg. No one knew he was there, fast asleep, except on occasion when someone accidentally trod on his trailing tail. In this way Freddy accompanied the family on a rare cinema outing to see 'Great Expectations'. As the blade dropped to the hero's neck in the final shot, I wished heartily for an instant that I, too, had a trouser leg to hide beneath.

Throughout my childhood years other animals came and went, some were very young, some sick or injured – monkeys galore, lemurs and bush-babies, serval cats and chimps, a baby hyena, a pangolin and a five-day-old elephant. All needed a great deal of understanding care and attention. Each added to the rich mix of experience and played their part in moulding my future. I had not realized until recently just how immensely significant that period in Africa had been.

I was fortunate having a father interested in sharing his wonder and curiosity of the living world. He took delight in showing my sister and me all manner of things, from carpenter wasps creating their nest to coaxing large, hairy trapdoor spiders out of their tunnels by gently scratching the trapdoor with a blade of grass; from explaining the behaviour of baboons to revealing, with a scalpel, what lay beneath the skin of a snake. I absorbed all he shared and this love of living things re-emerged in the healer I became in later life, as did the influence of my mother in her defiant stand against Apartheid.

A BRUSH WITH APARTHEID

'...Deep inside, in that silent place where a child's fears crouch...'
Lillian Smith
'The oppressed and the oppressor alike are robbed of their freedom.'
Long Walk to Freedom, Nelson Mandela

My early childhood in South Africa was a wonderfully rich and magical experience for me, but this perfect world was filled with cracks caused by witnessing the consequences of violence. It was the period when Apartheid was becoming established in the lead up to South Africa becoming a republic. Young though I was, I became aware of how much courage is needed to stand against self-serving systems that protect their own interests at the expense of others.

I was frightened and appalled by the level of animosity directed at my mother when, one day, a burly Afrikaner policeman strode up as we emerged from the local greengrocer. He stood menacingly close, his face thrust forward into hers and threatened her, punctuating each threat with a shove against her shoulder. My sister and I watched paralyzed with fear as our mother stood her ground. Finally, unable to intimidate her, the policeman spat in her face with the words "Kaffir boetie!" (Kaffir brother) and strode off.

My mother stood there shaking beside us with his spit dripping down her face. I watched it slide down her neck, in horror and revulsion. It was the first time I remember feeling completely helpless. Anger against the policeman and all he stood for came later, and lasted until the moment I watched Mandela make his inauguration speech on television.

My father had his own difficulties for refusing to teach in segregated classes at the Witwatersrand University. Recently, my sister unearthed an old photograph of my father as a vigorous young man striding out beside members of his faculty, marching in protest against Apartheid. I feel proud but also sad that I know so little about what he experienced both then and earlier in the war when he was part of the Resistance Movement in Denmark. He was always reticent about what happened and neither my sister nor I pressed him for details.

In 1959 our lives took a new direction. The trail of footprints I was following in South Africa came to an abrupt end. We were on six month's sabbatical leave in Europe when my father and mother heard that warrants for their arrest had been issued as a result of their stand against Apartheid. Members of my father's faculty had been arrested under the *ninety-day 'no trial'* Act. The law was being used as a sadistic form of persecution with people being re-arrested immediately on their release. Many were broken by the stress this practice caused.

This disturbing news forced the family to flee South Africa. By lucky coincidence my father had been offered a post in Uganda just before he heard about the warrants. He decided to accept. Leaving my mother in England with my sister and me, he went back to South Africa in secret, slipping over what was then the Southern Rhodesian border. With help and support of loyal friends, he packed what belongings he could, crated some of the animals we had accumulated and arranged to have them shipped out of the country without coming to the attention of the police. Everything else, including our house, was sold for a song to the tenants who had been looking after it while we were abroad.

Both my sister and I missed our old way of life and our friends - but the knowledge that our parents were safe softened the blow of leaving South Africa and helped us adjust to the new way of life.

Even though the trail I was following in South Africa ended unexpectedly, I found sufficient clues - such as the episode with the spitting policeman - to explain the direction my life took later on. Apartheid had left its mark. It was not possible as a small girl to witness the injustices and the angry despair of Africans under Apartheid rule without asking, Why? I never got any answers that made sense. One of the worst consequences was that Africans turned on each other in acts of aggression as the only way to release their fear and desperation. It was safer than attacking the cause of their misery.

I would stand watching from the doorway of the kitchen when locals brought anonymous Africans to the house for help. Sometimes they came with dreadful stab wounds, their faces grey, teeth chattering, their bodies in shock. Sometimes they came bleeding from the brutal beatings dealt out by the South African police and with deep puncture wounds from dog bites.

I saw the care taken by my mother and father as they wrapped victims in blankets and seated them by the kitchen range for warmth. My parents were my role models; their care and concern for Africans, their continuous protest against the social injustices of Apartheid, were an example to me of how we should support others struggling to survive within unfair systems.

My parents' reputation for caring and justice spread amongst the Africans. More and more turned to them for help. Some of them became such regulars we regarded them as friends – and Old May was one of these.

Old May was a familiar figure. Dressed in baggy shorts that were far too big for him and a khaki-coloured vest so full of holes it seemed pointless wearing it, he was easy to spot trotting amongst the blue-gum trees. Known locally as 'Bushman' for being short of stature, he would be absent for weeks and then suddenly arrive unannounced at the kitchen door looking for work. He would stand there with his pickaxe over his shoulder, a dark silhouette in the doorway, the light shining between legs bowed by early malnutrition. He was a cheery, chatty soul

with a dramatic flair in acting out for us the latest events in his life. My mother and father tried hard never to turn him away. They would find odd jobs for him around the garden – digging up tree stumps, turning over the rather neglected vegetable patch. He would wield his pickaxe with enthusiasm, bringing it down in a sweeping arc with an explosive pshooh! as the point buried itself in the ground. No one knew where Old May lived. It was assumed he found shelter in abandoned huts or beneath the roads in the large concrete drainage culverts that carried rainwater along the dongas in wet weather.

He arrived one day in his usual way but, on this occasion, his shoulders were slumped and his face sickly-grey with pain. In response to questions he inclined his head to reveal a long gash across his scalp; blood soaked down his back between his shoulder blades. He had been in an alcohol-fuelled fight at a local shebeen and been cracked over the head with a knobkerrie. Although not serious it needed treatment, but Old May was suspicious of the hospitals and refused to go. It fell to my mother to use all her skill in patching him up. As there was no sticking plaster, she finished by applying a lavish protective layer of scarlet nail varnish over the area.

It must have stung dreadfully but he did not flinch. As she finished, Old May cautiously explored the top of his head with tentative fingers. On seeing this, Letty, our housemaid, disappeared and returned with my mother's freestanding mirror to show him the result. He grinned with delight at his reflection. 'Haugh!' he exclaimed, examining the bright red slash across his dark pate. Then again, 'Heh!' as he turned his head to see it from the other side. As he disappeared into the evening gloom, the splash of scarlet bobbing along in the air was the last thing to disappear from sight.

Old May was a well-known face in Windsor Woods for several more years. Then one day there came disturbing news. He had developed a bad cough and had taken himself off to hospital. We knew this meant something was seriously wrong. My mother and father found him huddled, face to the wall, beneath the thin grey hospital-issue blanket. His eyes were dull and all the life had drained out of him. He spoke little and showed no interest in what was happening around him. He had TB. My parents stood beside him, uncertainly, then patted him on the shoulder and left again.

The last contact anyone had with Old May was to say goodbye as his coffin was lowered into the grave. My parents and a few African mourners said a prayer, sang a hymn and bade a final farewell before departing the bleak, lonely piece of waste ground that served as the African cemetery.

Reflecting on this period I realize how much I admire my parents in their stand against Apartheid. They have influenced the choice of activities of both my sister and I, and it feels as if this influence is strengthening rather than diminishing – especially in the area of social justice.

STANDING ALONE

'I am alone with the beating of my heart...'
Lui Chi
*'The events in our lives happen in a sequence of time, but in their
significance to ourselves, they find their own order...'*
Eudora Welty

Nothing in my African childhood prepared me for life in
an English boarding school. Although I had spent nearly
a year in England in 1958, becoming a boarder at a small
public school felt like the first real entry into the Western
world. As I write this I am aware of a deep reluctance to
think about it. I know I gained a great deal of benefit from
the experience and that there were happy moments, but my
overriding memories are unhappy ones.

The time leading up to it, in Uganda, had been vastly
different from South Africa - a wonderful but all too brief,
transitional time between being a *bush* child and having
to adapt painfully to an English way of life. Uganda was
exotically beautiful and opened a new world of adventure
and discovery for me. The climate was equatorial and
plants seemed to grow with indecent haste. For the first time
I experienced what it was like to live in a community and be
surrounded by other children.

It was also a time of living outside an apartheid system. Ugandans expressed themselves freely without fear. With no apartheid to repress or restrict them, they moved with confidence around their country. The only violence that touched our lives during that period was experienced second-hand through helping the stream of panic-stricken Belgian refugees fleeing from atrocities during the Congolese Uprising. But beneath the sympathy was the feeling that, to some extent, they were getting their just desserts. The Belgian colonialists had a reputation for brutal indifference towards the African population, not unlike that found in South Africa.

Uganda had brought one unpleasant change into my life. My sister and I were separated for the first time in our lives by the East African educational system. My sister at thirteen was sent off to boarding school in Kenya for secondary school education and I, at eleven, went to the local junior school in Kampala.

By the time I was ready to join her in Kenya, my father had been offered another post, this time at Ibadan University in Nigeria. With no satisfactory secondary schooling available there, our parents were forced to send us to be educated in England and, because of our different educational needs, this resulted, once again, in being sent to different schools.

On the never-to-be-forgotten day that I became a boarder, my mother drove through the school gates and parked under a large cedar tree. Cold February drizzle dripped down on us from the dark green needles overhead, grey dampness contrasting with the warm, vibrant colours of Africa that I had left behind. How I missed the golden grass, the red earth baking beneath a sky sun-bleached to pale denim.

It was the first time I had seen the school and I felt

intimidated by its imposing entrance and wide steps leading up to double doors. We were ushered into a side room just inside the entrance to await the Headmistress. We sat there by ourselves, silent, watched over by portraits of past headmasters with solemn expressions. Neither my mother nor I had anything to say in those miserable moments. The room was cold and felt unused; an impression, which was probably correct, as I never again entered this room in all the time I boarded there.

When my mother left an hour later, I stood on the steps beside the Headmistress overcome with the grief of parting. The searing pain of abandonment overwhelmed me, and I cried great gulping sobs as I watched the car disappear from sight. The last trace of her was the haze of exhaust fumes drifting between the gateposts. With my mother gone, I had to begin acclimatizing to the new system. This was the start of one of the worst and yet most influential periods of my life.

It was a shock being thrust into the form common room for the first time. The fuggy smell of stale air was layered with the aromas of damp clothing, food and cheap scent, suffused by the lingering smell of *Jeyes* fluid. Dingy grey-green lockers had been erected just inside the door intended to give privacy to the occupants but forming an oppressive barrier to the outside world. At first I hated those lockers but later came to appreciate them, as they would shield me from the eyes of patrolling teachers. I remember hiding behind them on wet Saturday afternoons, loath to go out, crouching out of sight with a book, a small transistor radio and a tin of sweetened condensed milk, its top punctured to dribble out the sweet and sticky contents.

The common room was a separate world ruled by wisecracking, foul-mouthed teenage girls. My life had hitherto been unsophisticated, living eight miles outside

Kampala town limits surrounded by African nature. I was used to living amongst people who were relaxed, colourful, felt enjoyment in simple things and laughed a lot. I had enjoyed outdoor tomboy pleasures and contact with the

natural world. Now I was challenged by sophistication. At first I felt totally out of my depth and unable to fend for myself, struggling to deal with the confusion I felt.

I learned what it meant to be marginalized. For the first time I came to appreciate the important lesson of accepting differences, something my parents had taught me in the difficult political climate of South Africa.

In addition, I began to realize how each of us develop personas to protect ourselves. In my form, there was gum-chewing Deidre. She was loud and more foul-mouthed than the rest. Ignoring me, she dominated the room with cynical banter, pausing long enough in her stream of talk to blow large pink bubbles, before continuing the flow of hard-boiled, sarcastic words. But over time I became aware her bluster and sarcasm was a protective front and perceived that she felt every bit as vulnerable as me. Once I realized that, I understood a warm-heart lay beneath her nut-hard shell. From then on I found her more likeable. It was a salutary lesson in looking below the surface that I never forgot.

The weather depressed me. The alien frigidity of the British climate matched public school life. I longed for Africa - the relaxed freedom I had felt in the heat. Nor could I get used to the spartan attitude that everyone else adopted to cold and discomfort. One of my vivid memories is of scurrying across the playground to the swimming pool before breakfast at the start of summer-term, my bare legs, mottled purple and covered in goose flesh. All of us stood shivering on the stone steps with towels wrapped across our chests, awaiting entry to the swimming pool. While some found this fun, I had memories of lying beside swimming pools soaking up the glorious African heat radiating off concrete paths.

The tracker in me, casting around for clues, picked up the trail again. Amongst the criss-crossing tracks of my experiences, one footprint stood out more clearly than the rest – that of the wounded healer, later to become one of my greatest allies.

Like the weather and being cold, there were many aspects of teenage life in Britain that I never adjusted to. My manners and vocabulary set me apart. As an adult I learned that subtle differences in table manners had singled me out. I folded my napkin on the 'wrong' side of the plate and tipped my soup bowl towards me rather than away. I had no experience of the lifestyle of the English middle class that the rest of my fellow classmates had in common. To them I must have appeared stupidly naïve, innocent, easy to tease and push around, placing me near the bottom of the pecking order. I was not alone, of course. There were others, outsiders like myself, who were marginalized. We befriended each other.

Some stood apart from the predatory pack, lovely souls liked by all, who flowed easily between groups, natural diplomats with nothing to prove. There was Katy, always kind, who somehow managed to steer attention away from us when baiting became too intense.

Despite the low rank I held amongst my peers, I rose to being elected *Form Rep* of the Lower Fifth girls in my second year. Though it carried some status, I suspect I got it purely on the grounds that no other girl wanted the bother. Still, my confidence rose with having prestige and, encouraged, I began to pay closer attention to my appearance. This was the time of Mary Quant with that chic, flat-chested, *Twiggy* look; a period of tight sweaters, mini-skirts and patent leather shoes. I spent birthday money on a couple of close-hugging jersey tops and wore them proudly. At fifteen I began to wear a bra. My first pair had conical shaped cups – the latest fashion from Marks and Spencer. They were decorated with concentric rings of stitching diminishing to a central bulls-eye at the tip. Being fashionably skinny, I had precious little with which to fill the AA cups. And that made me a target.

Entering the common room, back straight, deportment perfect, I was surprised to find an assembly of boys and girls. My heart did an uneasy jig of uncertainty as the handsomest boy in the form stepped forward to greet me. From the moment of my arrival, my heart an open flower, fluttering helpless and hopeless, had followed the sun of his godlike presence.

'Kirsten, as we feel you have done such a good job as our rep, the form wants to give you a small token of appreciation,' he said smiling. But his smile was crooked with anticipation - others were smirking too. With pompous ceremony, another boy stepped forward with a covered tray in his hands. A loud titter went round the room and a scorching wave of apprehension rose through me. This was likely to be moment of humiliation.

'Go on! Take off the towel,' everyone urged. The predatory air of a kill rose over the group. I was afraid to comply, equally I was afraid not to.

Reluctantly I lifted the cloth. On the tray was a collection of conical shaped salt-cellar tops. I stared at them without comprehension and stammered my thanks.

'We thought you might be able to use these,' said the boy.

All round the room form members were tittering, but I did not understand why until my golden god closed in for the kill. 'Something to fill that bra of yours!'

I fled the room.

For months afterwards, I walked hunched over wearing the biggest, baggiest jerseys I could find. The shame of being small-breasted lasted for years. It finally disappeared when my son was born. At last, in my thirties, I had a bosom to be proud of and could stand straight again.

This predatory pack instinct was not exclusively channelled towards pupils. Staff were singled out, too.

Because of their age and position, they had more weapons to fight back with – but sometimes the pupils emerged as the undisputed winners.

He was a small man with a grandiose name. A man who liked tweed jackets with padded shoulders that accentuated his meanness of height by making him appear almost as wide as he was tall. Did his parents sense he would be of little substance physically and try to make up for it?

He was enamoured of heavy brown leather shoes with steel heel protectors to slow down wear and tear. You could hear him coming along the concrete corridor, his thunderous footfall accompanied by the sharp ring of steel striking with every step. Close up there wasn't much to recommend him either. Fine brown hair carefully combed across his scalp topped a ruddy face dominated by a large mouth permanently pursed in disapproval. He was my least favourite teacher and taught my least favourite subject.

Yet he was liked by some - a woman teacher, for one. Stories about them circulated amongst the pupils. Our dirty little minds too easily pictured where she had been and what she had been doing, as we lay pillowed on our secret knowledge, eyes closed, listening to her quiet foot-fall progressing down the dorm towards her room each night after midnight.

The year I finally escaped boarding school, this teacher had the unenviable duty of being form master to the boys of my year. They mutually loathed each other and there was always a struggle for supremacy. Then came the time when he seemed to triumph. One of the boys had returned from Paris with large supplies of condoms and liquorice- flavoured roll–up papers. It was the 60s, the decade of free love and experimenting with hash. The forbidden booty was stashed behind the panels in the common room. They might have got away with it if others hadn't brought back toasters and kettles that overloaded the school's electrical circuitry. The resident caretaker, struggling to solve the problem of constantly blowing fuses, traced along the wiring and discovered the illicit stash.

Exposed at last, the boys were faced with their form-master's triumph and their own inevitable expulsion. The parents were informed and given the weekend to remove their sons. Before their departure, however, the boys found a way to retaliate.

While morning assembly was in progress, the excluded boys saw their chance to leave with panache. A few condoms had escaped confiscation. These were inflated with gas in the chemistry lab and tied, well out of easy reach, to the window grills facing the assembly hall. As staff and pupils exited the building, they came face to face with the jaunty condom balloons bouncing merrily in the breeze. The boys were gone. They had had the last word. The schoolmaster had the mortifying task of climbing a ladder to remove them – a job that took him all afternoon.

The mistress seemed affected too. She came in earlier after that.

Boarding school was when I really got to know the meaning of loneliness, but it was also when I began to understand the need for space and the value of time to be alone. This I found in the headmistress's private sitting room.

Miss Carter was an extremely perceptive woman who saw my struggle to fit in. I loved and trusted her. I think she would have made a wonderful mother yet she remained a spinster until her death. Perhaps in girls like me she found an outlet for her maternal nature. Naturally empathic, she saw and understood my need for homeliness. She recognized that I would benefit from breathing space away from the pack with its teenage competitiveness. Whenever she saw me struggling, she invited me to go and sit in her little room with a book. Sometimes she would join me with a cup of tea; occasionally, she let me watch TV as a treat.

I also found refuge in sickbay. Coming from the heat of Africa into the cold damp climate of England did not suit me; nor did the crowded, overheated fug of the common rooms. I developed chronic sinus problems and tonsillitis.

This made me a frequent visitor to the sanatorium. Very quickly I had spotted the opportunity for time-out presented by being sick, sometimes faking it to escape the hardness of pack life.

Still hunting for key elements in my healer's journey, I spot another footprint clearly defined amongst the others - my introduction to meditation.

Of any one thing I encountered at boarding school, meetings in silence had the most profound influence on me. It was my introduction to quiet reflection, and I liked the emphasis on looking for God within. I had never been able to relate to a distant God whose actions seemed capricious and judgemental, but I could relate to one that spoke within my heart, through my own conscience and inner knowing. Towards the end of my four years at the school, I began to look forward to those Sunday morning meetings. The practice of going within filled me with a peace that sustained me throughout the week.

Years later I would be introduced to other forms of deeper meditation.

My time in boarding school ended when an international school was completed within a mile of my parent's home in Nigeria. I left England and returned to complete my schooling in Africa. The atmosphere there was open, relaxed, the mix of nationalities, both of pupils and staff, making it easy-going and flexible. Learning became stimulating, an interesting mix of combined educational approaches from Britain, Sweden and America. It was the happiest period of my school life and, in spite of having to cram two years syllabus into one, I passed my exams and returned to England to enter a teacher's training college in Hampshire.

Recently I returned to my old boarding school. I went out

of curiosity to a reunion. It felt odd being there amongst old scholars from different forms; decent folk circulating the room with stolid, grey-weather piety, quite different from the exceptional rebelliousness and individual creativity expressed by members of my year.

Even as an adult I could feel my difference standing there amongst them. My separateness. I was not part of these people. It brought to the surface all the memories of early confusion about feeling marginalised; all the shame, the humiliation that accompanied it. It reminded me of the underlying question I had asked myself as a girl: If I am not part of these people, then who am I? Now I see it as part of my growth as an individual.

This phase of my life I have most difficulty in reviewing, knowing that my perceptions are probably distorted by my difficult experiences. Lurking, almost hidden from sight, the victim is there too.

FOOTSTEPS TO SELF-DISCOVERY

'We will discover the nature of our particular genius when we stop trying to conform to our own or other people's models, learn to be ourselves, and allow our natural channel to open.'
Shakti Gawain

'He who knows others is wise; he knows himself is enlightened.'
Lao-Tzu

'Always be a first rate version of yourself, instead of a second rate version of somebody else.'
Judy Garland

Four polite leaves of lettuce sat beside a quartered tomato; a spring onion edged away from staining contact with three beetroot slices. The potato salad, not fussy, turned pink at the edges whilst the cucumber - three slices - sat coolly alone like the spring onion. Heinz salad dressing, not mayonnaise or French dressing. White bread already buttered sat stacked on a separate plate.

High tea is a very British tradition, not something I was used to coming from Africa. I am not sure if it is a tradition that runs throughout English society but it was certainly common in the working class households I experienced in the late 60s, early 70s. There was a sort of unimaginative decency in the way the meals were presented – simple, direct gestures of what was thought of as responsible, wholesome family fare. I ate many plain, English working-class meals of the meat-and-two-veg and high-tea-salad variety in my early adult life. It was the result of a series of life choices I made at the time. Choices arising out of how I felt about myself.

One of the greatest challenges facing anyone is that of self-knowledge. Healers, too, have to face those areas in themselves that are not aligned with their inner-truth, and I am no exception. It was inevitable, therefore, that my footsteps led me along the path to self-discovery. I had to understand and accept myself before I could live my truth. Ultimately, true expression cannot be denied without consequences - understanding that can be really painful.

I had been unprepared for and never really adjusted to English boarding school education. My sister, already familiar with boarding school in Kenya, fared little better but, being two years my senior, was able to escape the sixth-form to attend a college in Oxford, boarding with a don's family until she had taken her GCE exams. She was interested in science subjects whereas I was of a creative bent. The result was that our lives continued to unfold in different directions. She went to university and I, more artistic but less academic than her, enrolled in the teacher's training college.

I was fired with idealism and visionary enthusiasm for bringing forth a generation of creative, freethinking, adventurous children. The reality, sadly, never matched the vision. My enthusiasm turned to disappointment and frustration, and I switched to teaching disadvantaged children (more about this in the following chapter). I taught in *Special Education* but discovered after several years that my heart was no longer in it, and I gave up. An avenue explored that turned out to be a dead end.

But none of it was wasted. Without realizing it, I was laying foundations for the healing work to follow. Everything, including what had begun as a bush-child's play, was part of a long apprenticeship that ended with the birth of my own child. There was so much to learn about life and how people operate in their lives. The many strategies they adopt to survive that compromise integrity. The phase of my life I describe next is a perfect illustration of this.

It was while I was at college that I had my first real relationships, and struggled through the mess and pain of broken-heartedness. I had already experienced the grief of being severed from my family and from my roots in Africa, but this was another level of emotional pain that undermined my confidence in myself. I felt inadequate and different, never quite coming up to scratch, as my mother would say. Once again I felt a misfit, longing only to belong. It was an echo from my school days but now more intense. Finally, I was rescued from my misery by a gentle working-class boy who took a shine to me. He was sweet-natured, not very exciting, but he loved me.

Now I made a discovery. If I lowered my sights, life became less challenging. My instinct to survive led me to a choice. I chose to shield myself from further pain by suppressing my individuality and emotions. Better half alive and numb than fully alive and unhappy. Warmly embraced by this homely, working-class family, I began adapting to working class life and their expectations of conformity. Mother Beel was mild, sweet-natured like her son, very proud of her husband and boys. Father Beel was solidly conservative in his values, a mason and proud of it.

I found myself enjoying the uncomplicated lifestyle that was offered. It also offered a chance to dress up for the Masonic Ladies' Night, wearing elbow-length gloves and a slinky, sateen ball dress. It was the time of hairpieces and every young woman had them. I had two that were curled at the hairdressers and attached on the day of the ball with a forest of pins and clips to transform me into a Grecian goddess.

At last I felt an easing of pressure, a respite from the emotional struggles that had been going on so long. It was safe. I believed that by staying within this framework I would be in control, be protected from the heartaches and feelings of inadequacy. I had found a niche and acceptance within a social group where I could succeed and shine.

Beauty muzzled with pain
Unable to express herself
Becomes tame, mundane.
What a shame.

This period of conformity continued for many years but there is always the time of reckoning. A moment comes of deep emotional crisis when our real voice demands to be heard. A decision has to be made – suppress once again or let the true self emerge. My day of reckoning came more than twenty years later by which time I was married to another gentle, thoughtful man whom I had met on holiday.

We started our life together living in a tiny flat, part of a terraced house in a humble street in East London. Tiny it may have been, but living there was filled with rich human experiences and remains memorable for a strange coincidence.

Mr Ringe lived next door, an old man surrounded by memories and memorabilia of his beloved wife, the most precious of which was her old grand piano. Though she had been gone twenty years or more, he kept it tuned and polished and once a week he played it, stumbling through the pages of yellowing music scores and picking out half forgotten melodies.

I used to lie in bed at the weekend listening to him playing. It became part of my Sunday morning wake-up ritual. Through the wall I could hear melodies tapped out, fumbling and hesitant at first, then picking up speed with confidence borne of remembrance. Notes became fluid, melodic, and the creaking rustiness of arthritic fingers recalling forgotten chords suddenly found their suppleness once more.

I got to know him over the back garden fence.

I couldn't have spoken to him more than a dozen times in all the time I lived at number 27, yet I gained a sense of a rich life that had been lived to the full and crammed with purpose descending into aching loneliness with the death of his wife. I left one day when he was out, to start a fresh life at 34, Geere Road, a small flat in Stratford, East London, and I did not go back for more than a year.

The flat was tiny - the upstairs half of a small terraced house - but I was blissfully happy in my own space and I might never have thought of Mr Ringe again if it had not been for a letter that arrived one morning. It was addressed to a Mr Philip Ringe. It looked official and had the address of an insurance company printed across the back flap. Could there be some connection with my old neighbour? I wondered. After all, the name was not that common and I remembered him telling me he was East London born and bred. On the strength of this reasoning, I visited him.

It was the first time I had set foot in his home and seen the beautifully maintained grand piano that took up half the reception room. On its glossy surface was a snow-white, crocheted doily upon which stood a vase of artificial roses. The keys were pure white ivory, too, in between the polished ebony. Not a hint of age marred their perfection. Mr Ringe turned the letter over in his hands and a half-grimace, half-smile crossed his face.

Philip, it turned out, was his estranged brother, several years deceased, and 34, Geere Road had been his old family home where he grew up. He opened the letter. It was an insurance policy that had matured into a considerable sum. Charles Ringe, now the only surviving member of the family, was the beneficiary.

To celebrate, a cup of tea was brewed and he talked about his working life with the sugar giants, Tate & Lyle, until his retirement when a huge party was thrown by the company in recognition of his years of loyal service. He waved at a framed black and white photo of himself receiving a large golden handshake from the company director. In the background a woman I identified as his wife beamed her pride and pleasure. She had been a celebrated concert pianist and life with her had been a wonderful whirl of concerts, functions and dinner parties. How he missed her. How he missed the dancing! The conversation lapsed into silence as he tapped into memories. Then he turned to me and surprised me with a question.

Would I mind very much if an old gentleman, such as he, had the temerity to ask me to be his dancing partner? Every few months The Odd Fellows, a Friendly Society to which he belonged, held a dance. He longed to go but felt inhibited by the lack of a partner. It would all be most proper, he assured me. No hanky-panky.

I was touched. Why not? Of course I would go. For three years, I partnered him to the dinner dances and it was a joy to see him with old friends smiling, laughing, reminiscing. He danced with me a little, holding me the correct distance from himself - the proper gentleman. He breathed heavily as he fumbled his way through half-remembered dances, his back stiff and his steps creaky. He smelled of Old Spice, his suit out of storage, of old man and mothballs.

Sadly, his balance was not what it once was so he was forced to give up. Instead he derived pleasure from watching me enjoy myself taking part in "excuse me" dances, whirling about the floor in the Military Two Step, quickstep and waltz.

There came a time when I became immersed in domesticity and an evolving relationship. Mr Ringe slipped into the background of my mind, until one day I felt prompted to contact him. A strange voice answered the phone.

Mr Ringe no longer lived there. He had passed away a few months before, I was told. So cut and dried. Uninterested. Hearing the young, professional-sounding voice, I knew that the house had been transformed. I imagined modern décor with repro pictures on the wall, a coffee table standing in the place of that beautiful grand piano. All traces of the old man swept away.

From my contacts I was able to glean that he had died after a short illness. I felt a mixture of guilt and deep sadness that I hadn't seen him again. I found comfort in knowing that Tate & Lyle had given him a wonderful send off and the Odd Fellows had turned out in force. Still, I would love to have been there to celebrate a life so well and vibrantly lived.

I loved the gritty humour and unsophisticated directness of East Enders. They called a spade a spade. No messing. So different from the sophisticated courtesies of my own background that took you round the houses and back again before arriving at what was meant.

My husband and I spent nearly twenty happy years together, much of it in the working-class suburbs of East London. But the choice I had made years before to protect myself was lurking like a time bomb, waiting for something to trigger the fuse. The countdown began when events brought me into contact with the world of psychics and healers.

Quite unexpectedly, I developed high blood pressure. Barbara, a fellow teacher, offered me healing that I gratefully accepted, as an alternative to pills. Suddenly I found myself reconnected to the subtle and mysterious realms of the numinous. My early, inexplicable childhood experiences, that had been buried for so long, came rushing to the fore. I thirsted to learn more, knowing instinctively that this would offer me a way to express myself. Teaching was no longer enough. I joined my healer friend, entering the world of mediumship and healing that has become my life's work - a different world where intuition, sensitivity and awareness are paramount, superseding reason and intellectual rationalizing. The following story illustrates this.

The crowd gathered at the entrance of Wanstead Cemetery to celebrate Jadwiga's life, the attire jazzy, mood determinedly bright; forty single red roses clutched in perspiring hands; red as Jadwiga's blood so needlessly spilled in a motor accident on a beautiful tree-lined avenue. This was her day, a celebration of her short life as she was laid to rest with quiet simplicity. The atmosphere was resolutely upbeat but a random glance left and right revealed many faces inward-looking, some sombre, some reflective. Muted flutters of conversation and gentle laughter could be heard as people moved on cue towards the parked cars behind Penny and Vitek, Jadwiga's parents, pausing briefly to drop their farewell rose on top of her coffin. Quiet groups waited, watched Penny gently lay a lone bouquet of flowers in the boot of the car as if she were laying her beloved daughter down to sleep.

At the family home, the mourners gathered in the garden, clustered beneath shady trees to avoid the fierce sun. Soft ribbons of laughter threaded in and out amongst hollyhocks and fuscia bushes in the well-tended flowerbeds. Penny, brittle-bright in her grief, moved doggedly from group to group, the perfect hostess, offering sandwiches and refills of tea.

While listening to polite conversation, I heard another voice insistently demanding my attention about some flowers. It was a voice I could not place at once. Puzzled I looked round to find the source but there was no one there. Suddenly I realized I was listening to Jadwiga saying urgently, 'Please tell Mama that my flowers are dying. It's too hot there. Tell her before they die.'

I whispered Jadwiga's words into Penny's ear. She exclaimed, 'Oh my God, I've forgotten to take Yadja's flowers out of the car.' She thrust the tray into my hands and returned a moment later with the bouquet of wilting flowers within the cellophane wrapping. But Penny was transformed. Gone was the brittle brightness. Now her face glowed and she radiated a deep joy as she moved once more from group to group.

As I left the Lanowski home an hour later, I spotted the flowers - now lovingly arranged - standing proudly upright in a vase. Jadwiga's message had got through to me just in time.

I learned many things of which I had no previous experience - that there are numerous ways to tune into subtle realms of intuition as a means of expanding awareness. The old-fashioned method of divination – scrying - is one. Most people are familiar with stories of gypsy women gazing into crystal balls or at tea-leaves at the bottom of a cup, but in fact anything can be used as a focus.

I tried my hand at sand reading. The *sitter* (for whom the reading was being done) drew a pattern in sand and then I 'read' the bumps and squiggles imprinted in the sand. Of course, I wasn't actually seeing what I spoke of but gazing at the lines enabled me to slip to another level of awareness. A good example of this was my reading for a woman I will call Diane. Rather than draw anything, she placed both hands on the tray of sand, pressed, and then added three dots in the centre of one palm print. I gazed down at the sand and let my mind drift as I had been taught to do, relaxed my eyes so everything became slightly out-of-focus. At first, all I was conscious of was two handprints and three dots but gradually I felt something else being suggested. It felt like there should be four dots, not three. Then it occurred to me that I was looking at three people. I finally started speaking.

'I see three people here but I feel there should be four. Why is that?'

Diane replied that she was one of four children. The fourth, a boy, had died in his teenage years as a result of a tragic mis-diagnosis at the hospital. With this response, a doorway was opened in me. Suddenly I saw a whole series of events in the handprints before me and, in speaking of them, I found that three-quarters of what I had said was meaningful in some way for Diane.

Flower claire-sentience was another avenue for developing intuition explored. It is amazing how going into the garden and breaking off a small branch or a flower can provide an in-depth intuitive reading. Angela presented me with a rose bud she had brought for a reading. Where she had broken it off the main stem there hung a long thin thread of outer stalk. She had snapped off all the thorns for easy handling. I let my mind relax. All I was conscious of were these two facts. I felt she had entered life with difficulty - that she clung to a thread of life for her first year. This was true. She was premature and it was touch and go whether she lived. Four thorns had been broken off. I felt they represented four major crises in her life but on each occasion she had been protected and everything had turned out well. This also turned out to be true.

Psychometry held a great fascination for me. Objects carry the vibrational imprint of the owner and hold the echoes of events and strong emotions. Occasionally, psychometry is called into use by the police in an attempt to solve a puzzling disappearance case, particularly when there is an absence of clues. In this exercise, sensing information about the owner is the purpose.

I will never forget the first time I tried to read an object without knowing the owner. After holding the object - a front door key - and tuning in for a few minutes, I asked myself what sort of person owned this key. I discerned a restless energy quite unlike my own, a rather tumultuous series of emotions threaded through with a lot of laughter. It felt feminine. Suddenly I had a hunch that this person really loved fairy tales. Russian fairy tales. In fact one in particular, *Baba Yaga*.

It turned out that the key's owner was the daughter

of our teacher, a restless, lively person who loved a good laugh. I was immensely surprised when she said that her favourite story was the Russian folk tale about the witch, *Baba Yaga*. She reached into her bag and drew out her key-ring. Dangling from it was a charm. It was a witch seated in a mortar, using the pestle as an oar - *Baba Yaga*!

More than anything else, we practised developing the 'seeing' gift, clairvoyance. It is a gift that comes and goes for me. I get flashes of clairvoyance for long periods and then it goes dormant again. I never know for certain when it will return but, when it does, it is triggered by need and usually to benefit someone who has approached me for healing.

Informative though these exercises were, they were not, in the majority of cases, particularly profound. My interest waned. I was not interested in using these gifts to entertain or impress others.

It was Jadwiga's mother, Penny, who especially influenced my thinking in those early days of exploration. Through her I started to think about such radical ideas as the nature of reality and how we create our lives. Through discussion we explored the idea that our beliefs create our reality, that we are not at the mercy of the past, that the point of power is in the present and that we can heal the past from the present by changing our beliefs. It filled me with excitement.

She introduced me to concepts and thoughts that none of the other mediums and healers considered at all. Their metaphysical understanding fell broadly within *Spiritualism* where the intention is to prove survival after death. Many attended meetings for the comforting knowledge that death was not the final destination, just a portal to another world. But you only need to get proof of survival once - as Penny had had through my relayed message from Jadwiga. The rest were mainly interested in getting their problems sorted, and life is not about surrendering your responsibility to make decisions.

Psychic gatherings in the East End of London were largely attended by people who could not be described as deep-thinkers. The information from the 'other side' went unquestioned, and I soon found this unsatisfying. I needed more intelligent discussion and conversations with Penny went part of the way. She stretched me, made me want to understand more about the subtle aspects of the reality we live in and, more importantly, the nature of my own personal reality.

It was after my son was born that I turned to the world of healing and a much more subtle dimension of creative awareness opened up before me. It connected me to energies that were truly transformative in their nature and required a different level of personal mastery and responsibility. I opened a healing and development circle and before long there were nine regular members. Every week we practiced meditation, gave each other healing and sent absent healing to a list of people who had requested help. It ran once a week for five years until my husband found a job in the West Country. It was a sad day when we held the closing circle. In tears, we hugged each other for the final time knowing that life was going to feel very different from then on. We had grown in our healing work together, explored ideas and discussed insights - but I knew it was time to move on.

The move to Bath proved very stimulating. I found myself surrounded by a number of interesting and gifted people. They were visionaries, original thinkers on the cutting edge of metaphysics and quantum science. And most were healers in some capacity. These people were *New Agers* who had come of age - what I would call *heavyweights* in spiritual thinking. Personal responsibility and self-growth was the chief focus. For the first time I felt truly surrounded by peers who spoke the same language as me. We thought the same way, were interested in the same subjects, and entertained concepts beyond the range of most people. I was truly happy for a time, but it did not last. My time of reckoning was finally at hand. I could no longer suppress who I was.

I began to feel restricted, constrained by the life of diminishing vision that I was leading. I could no longer deny that for me spirituality and healing were all important. My marriage began to fail because of our differing needs. There was a great deal more to life than I was able to tap into within the marriage – an enormously exciting and subtle area offering potential for expansion. I knew without doubt this was important for me. The time bomb finally exploded and I left my marriage to pursue what I saw as my calling. At last I began to live my own truth and in the process started a new phase of my life. It was an enormously painful period that I return to briefly in a later chapter. I emerged from it able to help countless others through the same crisis of being true to themselves.

Thinking back, I can see that I came from one background, the cultured academic world, and spent a period exploring another - life in the London East End. Ultimately I discovered I did not belong in either. Again I found myself in the position of not belonging anywhere, but this time I was not afraid. Conforming within what was considered the norm was not for me and I realised that being different was not something of which to be ashamed.

Within this spiritually focused life I have been able to create a unique position for myself; one created out of all the things that matter to me. A system of values, ethics, beliefs within which I can express myself with confidence; where I can mix together with others without feeling a need to belong. Being different, I discovered, has given me a great advantage. I am not hampered by the restrictions imposed by social groupings and their various codes of conduct.

I have created a position of my own, one where I can move throughout the layers of society and be accepted by all. As others put it, I have become a cross-cutting tie. It is an anthropological term used to describe those who cut across allegiances and create connections that are not normally made, connecting groups together who normally don't associate.

DAMAGED LIVES

'Sell your cleverness and buy bewilderment.'
Rumi
*'A well-developed sense of humour is the pole that adds
balance to your steps.'*
William Arthur Ward

Having difficulty in communicating our feelings and our needs is common to many of us. It was teaching young people with damaged lives that provided profoundly useful experience, helping me gain insight into the different problems that can arise. It showed me how important it is to be able to express feelings and clarify what is going on inside, not just for others but also for our own benefit. For the first time I fully understood the link between self-expression and self-esteem. Everything I learned during this period was later put to use in my healing practice.

I had become a schoolteacher by default. Academically, I wasn't geared for university and being a teacher linked me with academia enough to satisfy the family. I opted for the state educational system, believing it would give me enough space to express myself imaginatively and creatively. My dream was to encourage individual potential and watch it blossom. As a result of my own educational experiences, I felt empathy with others who lacked confidence and success. I wanted them to succeed and rise in their own esteem.

For most of my early life I was deluded into thinking it was unsafe to show ignorance. It meant being an imbecile. My poor father unwittingly made me feel this by letting me *help* him mark his students' work. Too young to go to school like my sister, I had yet to form friendships and receive invitations to play as she did. Bored, I hovered round him whining, wanting him to play.

My father, struggling to mark stacks of student papers, drew me to him, set me on his lap and told me I could help him mark the papers. I watched round-eyed as he scored red lines through long paragraphs, saying, 'Stupid! That's absolutely wrong! You know better than they do. You are a clever girl aren't you?' Of course I wanted to be a clever girl so I became very adept at hiding the fact that quite often I had no idea what he was talking about. Not knowing was not safe. I lived in dread of that red line through my own work and being called *stupid* in that scathing tone.

This, and the experiences that followed at boarding school, were powerful influences in the choices I subsequently made. As a newly qualified teacher I looked for posts in less affluent areas and found one in Barking, a staunchly working class borough, on the eastern edge of Greater London. It was a good position and I gained much through working alongside a teacher trained in Rudolf Steiner education. He was a skilled storyteller and I would listen to him on Friday afternoons narrating powerful sagas of heroic deeds and epic voyages to transfixed children. It gave me an inkling of the power of story. Years later, I found a use for storytelling in the form of creative visualizations. This enabled clients to tap into their own hidden depths for the answers they needed.

But teaching in Barking did not satisfy me for long. The classes were too big. I wanted something smaller, more intimate. Unconsciously imbued with my mother's passionate support of the underdog, I decided to use my teaching skills to help the disadvantaged. Week after week, I scanned the columns in *The Times Educational Supplement* for something that would offer me an opportunity, eventually finding an educational post at an assessment centre for court-referral cases. These were children who had committed crimes or who had been removed from dysfunctional homes. Many fitted into both categories. All were boarders. All were disturbed, many aggressive, and all had low self-esteem. Within me rose an urge to *mend* their fractured lives and situations, so I applied and was appointed.

Looking back, I can see that I had something important to offer - a sensitivity born out of that sense of not belonging. I recognised the hunger of the human heart; a hunger that crosses all social divides throughout the broad spectrum of society. Being able to make those young people feel both heard and understood was a gift of mine. It brought me satisfaction and, in a strange way, I felt heard too and this dissolved some of my own painful memories from the past.

In the assessment centre my creative and imaginative skills were put to good use as a way of developing a sense of achievement in the children. Remembering what I had discovered at the previous school about the power of story, I made a practice of reading and telling stories to my classes. It was deeply satisfying and for some of the children immensely therapeutic.

Lorna was big-boned, tall for her age. Everyone who did not know her thought she was in her late teens and treated her accordingly — even the justice service. She wasn't. She was thirteen and emotionally much younger, and prone to violent tantrums to get her way. Her reasoning was simple - if she wanted something she took it. If thwarted she would turn violent towards whoever or whatever stood in her way. Lorna had strength that matched her size. She could cause a lot of damage when in a rage, which is what led her to being incarcerated on many occasions in her own cell in Holloway Prison for women.

The records chronicled her sad life of being frequently 'banged up' with women criminals, reports of arson, grievous bodily harm, car thefts and muggings. Aware of her reputation, I was naturally nervous of her temper and never felt completely at ease in her presence. I needed to be in control but I was fearful of thwarting her, not wishing to become one of her casualties.

In spite of this, I liked Lorna. There was something terribly tragic about this emotionally stunted girl with massive self-inflicted injuries scarring both forearms, and I spent a lot of time trying to find ways to enrich her experience. I had no real success, however, until I learned to handle her rages.

Inevitably, I found myself facing her in a conflict of interests, mouth dry, heart pounding madly. She decided she wanted to go to Australia to look for her birth mother and, having made the decision, she wanted to leave immediately - in the middle of the lesson! The more I tried to reason with her the more rapidly her frustration mounted. Her fingers gripped tightly the back of a chair, surrounded by the chaos she had created - upturned desks, thrown pens, torn books, the fragments of a smashed vase. A jam jar of red paint that she had hurled at the wall trickled down looking unpleasantly like blood.

Inspiration came at the height of my desperation. 'If you want to go,' I said, 'you'd better find out a bit about Australia. You'll want to know what to do when you get there.' My eyes had fallen on a slim volume of Aboriginal stories. I grabbed it and opened it at random. It was a myth about the kookaburra. 'Do you know what a kookaburra is?'

Lorna continued glowering but I could tell her interest had been caught. For a few minutes more the tension continued and then, suddenly, her fingers relaxed and, with a swift stride across the room, she grabbed the book. I flinched, thinking she was going to hit me with it. Instead she thrust it into my hands. 'Read it to me!'

This was my opportunity to defuse the situation. I pulled up a couple of chairs, opened the book, and read in a loud voice so that the children who had shrunk back against the walls during the fracas could listen too.

Lorna pulled her chair forward beside me so that she could look at the pictures while I read. She listened, rapt, absolutely absorbed in the story and, by the end, she was nestled up against me, her head on my shoulder, her thumb in her mouth, a picture of the emotional three-year-old she really was. I never had trouble with her again.

After watching a film recently, I found myself being drawn into the anger and frustration expressed by a black youth leader struggling to keep his young charges away from gang life and crime. Temporarily, I was thrown back into the despondency I had felt as a teacher struggling to bring meaning and value into the lives of those no-hope children caught up in the court and social service system. Crime was the only way they knew how to find status and that feeling of belonging. The same was true for Zak.

Zak, like Lorna, was one of those children. The same age, but as slight of frame and tiny as Lorna was large and heavy boned. Zak was another one of the expendables, a thrown-away child disowned by his parents. His angel face and long curls belied the fact that he had well developed criminal tendencies, and was worldly-wise well beyond his years. He was one of the 'Piccadilly Boys', a rent boy. A successful one, I heard.

Like most children at the assessment centre, he was difficult to contain when he felt the urge to go. There was the time he ran away to Piccadilly, no doubt wanting to top up his spending money. On this occasion he must have been out of luck. Hungry and without money, he began to think of the assessment centre — food and a warm bed suddenly seemed infinitely more appealing than sleeping rough in a doorway. But how was he to get back? It was a good twelve miles from the City.

From various accounts I pieced together what happened. Zak made his way to Whitechapel and somewhere near London Hospital he spotted a double-decker bus. It was empty, the keys still in the ignition. Zak, with adolescent confidence and no imagination for the possible consequences, hopped into the driving seat and stole the bus.

My own imagination fails when trying to visualise what happened next. He managed, somehow, to handle the wheel and reach the pedals of so large a vehicle by standing all the way. A police car chased after him. The route from Whitechapel to Romford is a straight run, so tricky negotiation of bends was not an issue, but slowing down obviously was as he trundled in second gear through every red light he came to. More police cars joined in the chase keeping their sirens on to alert other road users. Through Bethnal Green, Stratford, Forest Gate and Ilford, the cavalcade continued without mishap until the moment of reckoning finally came at a big roundabout on the edge of Romford. This marked the end of the straight run, as decisively as the stop beneath an exclamation mark.

Zak finally found his driving skills inadequate. Unable negotiate the curve, he took the only escape route available and drove the bus straight down the pedestrian underpass.

He arrived back at the centre unscathed and in time for supper, but the bus was a write-off and took two weeks to dig out.

I taught at the assessment centre for four years - four long years of giving everything I had. It was easy to get burned-out in that sort of work and I was on the edge. But there was another important reason for leaving.

Like the youth leader in the film, I had often felt my efforts were wasted because no one out there cared enough or understood the problems created by social inequalities. I, too, was in danger of viewing the world from the cynical and distorted perspective that both staff and pupils shared. *Out there* was a hostile and dangerous world. I watched the frustration of colleagues give way to hardboiled cynicism as a way of protecting themselves from the heartache of the situations they dealt with. Saddened and dismayed, I took a year out of teaching to replenish my empty batteries by doing an advanced diploma in art education.

I returned to teach in another area of disadvantage – with

children who had serious mental and physical handicaps. Many had profound communication problems being unable to speak and articulate their needs.

It was while teaching these children that my colleague gave me healing for high blood pressure and invited me to join the psychic development circle. Before long my thoughts turned to how to I could use my expanding abilities for the benefit of the children. By intuiting what the children had difficulty communicating, I would be able to meet their needs and so I embarked on my first conscious footstep towards becoming a healer. Teaching had joined forces with intuition.

With the aid of the psychic development exercises, I quickly developed the awareness needed to assist these profoundly handicapped - though mobile – youngsters. Not surprisingly, I found myself in joint charge of those who were (in those days) termed severely subnormal. I was partnered with an experienced teacher dedicated to this area of work.

He was a firm believer that, if given the opportunity to take the children away from their families for one week, he would be able to draw out of them abilities that no one knew they had. But it was over a year before we were entrusted with taking the children away to a centre near Southend in Essex. They blossomed. Their abilities expanded as they met new challenges and encountered new experiences. Suddenly the lumps of human dough emerged as personalities. They never looked back.

Twelve children shuffled with ungainly steps towards the bus. A few faces, our 'clever ones', registered delighted comprehension. The seaside! We are going to the seaside! They were the first to the bus impatiently brushing aside the helpful hands of the assistant. The gestures said, 'Leave me. I can do it by myself.'

Alf smiled, the smug smile of someone who had been proved right.

At the rear, I walked slowly holding Brian's hand, guiding his footsteps - I was his eyes - supporting his weight as he leaned heavily against me. His steps were crabbed and hesitant. I leaned closer to his hearing aid. 'We are going to the seaside, Brian. The seaside.' I put all the excitement and joy I could into my voice. 'The seaside!' I repeated, my mouth close to his ear.

Brian tilted still further his already up-tilted face, his expression blank. He squinted along his up-turned nose through the pebble thick glasses held in place with elastic tape. It was the only way he could see anything. He had seriously impaired eyesight.

'Ugh!' he grunted, and then more forcefully a second time, 'Ugh!' It was Brian's way, his only word of communication. Perhaps he had understood. I could not tell from his face, but he ground his teeth - his sign of expectation.

The ride was short. Unlike most school buses the atmosphere was quiet. Most children sat stolidly looking at the back of the seat in front. Just a few squeals of delight reached the front where I sat with Brian. One word badly articulated, only just discernable, could be heard. 'Seaside!' The bus drew alongside the ramp down to the small beach and the children clambered out under supervision of four carers. Once again I brought up the rear with Brian.

Slowly we made our crab-like descent down the ramp to the beach itself. It was difficult to hold Brian. I could see he understood by the way he sniffed the air and flapped his free hand. As his feet reached sand, Brian started tearing at his clothes.

'No Brian. Not yet. Wait. Soon Brian.'

But Brian found new strength. He knew what to do at the seaside. He thrust away my restraining hands and tore off his T-shirt and baggy shorts. He would not be thwarted. It was the first time any of us had seen Brian undress himself. There he stood naked in his sandals, a stocky little figure looking out to sea, oblivious of the sharp breeze whistling round him and the stares of trippers.

'Ugh!' he grunted, shuffling towards the sea and tugging hard against my grip. He was too strong for me. As the first wave washed

over his feet, he sat down heavily on the sand. Before I could stop him, his hearing aids were flung in one direction, his glasses in another. The carers and I scrambled wildly to recover them. It was so unexpected. He had done this before. He obviously knew the full ritual of preparation for a swim – removing glasses and hearing aids was part of it. As the carers and I splashed back to the beach, Brian, already covered in strings of seaweed brought in on the tide, sat unconcerned in the waves in complete rapture, dribbling sand over himself.

He knew what to do at the seaside, and he was loving it.

PROGRESS OF A PILGRIM HEALER

'The eyes of my eyes are opened.'
e.e. cummings
*'When our eyes see our hands doing the work of our hearts, the circle
of Creation is completed inside us, the doors of our souls fly open,
and love steps forth to heal everything in sight.'*
Michael Bridge
*'Symptoms are a way for your body to say "Listen to me
talk for a change." '*
Carl A. Hammerschlag

There is a moment in every healer's life when they are
faced with the evidence of healing and the undeniable fact
that they have *the gift*. So it was with me. I moved to a new
neighbourhood, into a large, solidly built house in a quiet,
leafy suburb on the outskirts of London. It was a respectable
area that exuded an air of prosperity and conservative
security. I had no interest in being anything other than a
young mum, yet, within a week of moving in, my life as a
healer began.

*I stood at the window, with my young son in my arms, extending his
vocabulary, 'Look at that shiny sports car coming out of that garage,
Kieran. Brrm! Brrm! The man is going to work.' Seeing everything*

afresh as if through my son's eyes. So different. Such a contrast! What a long way this alien world was from that of my African childhood.

To overcome my feelings of being an outsider, I set myself the task of getting to know my neighbours up and down the street. Having a young toddler provided me with the excuse to walk slowly, stopping to show him things along the way, talking to people passing by.

This was how I met Dorothy.

She was cutting the hedge bordering the pavement, with the slow, laborious movements of the elderly. The shears, too heavy for her, drooped in her hands between each cut, the sound of her breathing loud in the pauses. Perspiration filmed her forehead; her skin that had been hidden beneath the genteel layer of foundation was exposed in mottled patches where she had mopped her brow. She stopped and smiled sweetly down at my son who gripped the wrought iron gate with his chubby little fingers. He surveyed the well-stocked flowerbeds neatly contained behind scalloped brick edging.

'Flower!' he announced, laboriously enunciating the new word.

'Clever Boy! Red flower.'

We introduced ourselves and talked about her garden.

'It is hard to maintain now that I have got arthritis in my fingers. Oh the joys of getting old!'

Impulsively, perhaps rashly, I said, 'I'm told I have the gift of healing.'

Instantly she extended her hands, knobbly with unsightly arthritic spurs, across the garden fence. She said, 'In that case, you can practice on me any time you want.'

This was my first chance to use healing outside of healing circle and it brought to the surface the fears that it might all be an illusion; that I had no special gift. I might fail, disappoint Dorothy and look a fraud. But there was no going back and, at the appointed time, I duly turned up and concentrated on being as open a channel as possible.

As commonly experienced, we both felt a sense of great wellbeing and emotional warmth bordering on love by the end of the session. After a cup of tea, I left, feeling that at the very least Dorothy was in a psychologically better space than when I had arrived.

A week later, Dorothy hailed me as I walked past her house. She behaved rather oddly, running her hands through her hair and patting her cheek as she talked, all the time smiling hugely. Suddenly, I realized why. Her fingers were definitely less knobbly. The bony spurs had diminished.

I stared, unable to believe my eyes. It did not seem possible. One week! They had dramatically reduced in one week!

In that instant I knew that healing really worked.

What makes a person a healer?

I believe that healing is an extension of the natural human capacity to love. Everyone can develop this capacity if they wish but certain people access it more easily than others. Healers have differing abilities. Some may be more effective with physical ailments, others with psychological or emotional issues. Then there are those who focus specifically on helping people to grow spiritually as a part of their healing.

Healers are naturally empathic. It is empathy that acts as the switch that *turns on the flow*. At some point in their lives, nearly everyone has experienced their heart going out to another in the desire to help. The compassion someone feels when putting their arms around another to comfort, falls within the frequency of energy transmitted through a healer. In the act of comfort, healing flows.

As with many novice healers, faced with the evidence of my 'gift', I became ultra-enthusiastic, wanting to practise, practise, practise, as fascinated by the results as the people who came. But something else occurred too. I was flooded with love during each healing session. Nothing else came close to providing me with a comparable experience - or the level of fulfilment.

I was hooked.

This all happened twenty-eight years ago in London. It was followed by a steady progression in healing and personal development that absorbed and fascinated me. I became increasingly aware of a sense of presence during the healing sessions - of being surrounded by entities invisible to my eyes but whose assistance and support was palpable. At first excited and awed, I came to expect them being with me through every healing session. It was a partnership, with me acting as a conduit - or channel - for their energy.

Healing became more subtle, the results less obvious and all too often, unexpected. The honeymoon period was over. It was hard to accept that people died in spite of my efforts - humbling. I had to learn to trust that sometimes death is the most appropriate outcome for the person involved.

As my experience grew, I noticed how economical the invisible realms are with time and energy. Batches of people showed up with the same physical ailments – groups of people like Dorothy with arthritis. A run of clients came with eyesight problems, or breathing difficulties, or breast cancer.

People were coming with complaints that revealed similar emotional problems and mental turmoil. I struggled at first, feeling a fraud, as I repeated the same words of counsel, the same message of encouragement to a dozen people, pinpointing the nub of their dilemma with ease. Then it dawned on me that the unseen realms were ensuring that all those who needed the same advice came together. That way, I didn't have to switch from one condition to another. I got used to people saying it was as if I was inside their heads, inside their lives.

It became clear over time that many of my own issues were being mirrored back to me in the people who came. I explored deeper and deeper into the miracles that were happening all around me, in the lives of others and in my own life. I learned about myself, resolved internal conflicts and grew as a person. Increasingly, I became aware that my gift in healing is more about expanding people's awareness than about curing ailments – although the latter was a frequent outcome.

From the outset, *Bach Flower Remedies* and their subtle yet powerful healing effects were a source of fascination. I had always been aware of how deeply affected I was when surrounded by nature. It was a habit of mine, as a child in South Africa, to walk through the eucalyptus woods when upset. A feeling of peace would be restored. Studying the flower essences, I learned how each plant restored balance in a wide range of psychological and emotional problems. It made sense to mix flower remedies for people to take home following the hands-on healing, and so began the combined discipline approach that became a feature of my practice in later years.

My healing took a new turn when we moved to Bath in 1988. I trained in aromatherapy massage and before long was thinking of the qualities of essential oils. In addition to their commonly known uses, I reasoned they had to have subtle effects similar to *Bach Flower Remedies*; ones that could be energetically transmitted when applied in a massage. For ten months I quietly researched, focusing on each essence in turn. The first was black pepper. I *tuned in* and before long got the impression that it was a *threshold* essence, a *procrastination buster.* It is difficult to explain how this information came to me but the simplest way is to say that I had a vision. In it I watched a man about to make his first fire-walk. He was fearful, hesitating, wondering if he should do it or not. Suddenly he found the resolve and stepped forward onto the coals. Simultaneously, I felt the black pepper's galvanizing qualities. I could sense hesitation melting away.

This discovery was put to the test when a fellow therapist suffering with leg problems came for a treatment. It transpired in the initial consultation that she wanted to launch herself in a new direction but was scared to take the plunge. I asked if she minded me testing my theory about black pepper. Happily she obliged. Into almond oil I mixed black pepper with a little lavender - well known for its calming, balancing benefits - and began to massage her legs gently. The result was dramatic. Uncharacteristically, my client broke the silence and talked solidly throughout the remainder of the session. Ideas spilled out of her, as she became more and more excited. Instead of lying relaxed at the finish, she jumped off the couch. Her procrastination was over and she could not wait to get started. She never looked back.

Satisfied that I was correct, I wrote in my notes: *BLACK PEPPER – for procrastination, moves situations on, the perfect 'threshold' oil for transformation, helps when feeling stuck and indecisive, helps with deep insight into what's holding you back.* By the end of a year I had a glossary of oils and their psycho-spiritual benefits, and started practising *esoteric aromatherapy.*

Recognizing that everything is connected on a subtle level - even thought - I was not surprised to find out that one of the great minds in the aromatherapy world, Patricia Davies, had done her own investigation and written a fascinating book called *Subtle Aromatherapy*. It was a much better term than *esoteric aromatherapy*. Less clumsy.

But I did not stop at working with the glossary. I started experimenting in dowsing oils. To begin with, the pendulum dangled stationary until I requested an indication for *yes*. Immediately, I felt a pulsing tingling in my fingers and the

pendulum swung into clockwise rotation. Then I asked for *no*. Once again the tingling pulse and this time the pendulum swung counter-clockwise. I checked these findings then, satisfied with my indicators, I began. I held the client's right hand, turned away so that I could not see them, and settled to watch the pendulum. While they touched each of the oils in turn I watched the pendulum's response. With a negative response they moved to the next oil and so on until the pendulum began to shift its swing. 'Yes!' I said as the pendulum swung into clockwise motion. The client lifted the oil out of the box.

We continued like this until all the oils that were required had been selected. These oils were dowsed a second time for the number of drops needed, then blended with almond oil and applied as a massage.

Dowsing oils and discussing their qualities was often highly effective for highlighting the deeper issues behind problems, and particularly useful for clarifying the main issue where the person felt confusion. The reported benefits received through subtle aromatherapy showed it to be far more powerful than those experienced through traditional methods.

I discovered, when healing, that standing back from my clients and working in the energy field also had a more powerful effect. Contrary to what might be expected, the energy appeared to get stronger when I stood a few feet away from the client. Varying the distance produced different effects and benefits. I had strange sensations in my fingers and palms when I moved my hands through client's energy field, a sensation of falling in love with parts of the body that had blocked energy. It would intensify for a time and then stop when balance was restored, leaving me free to move on.

Sometimes I had the urge to flick my hands, which made me very self-conscious, and I hoped fervently that my client would keep their eyes shut. It seemed so flaky. However, my confidence grew as clients started to report different sensations - a rush of heat or flow of energy accompanied by a sense of wellbeing. In general, they felt lighter in mood, happier. Occasionally they would refer to a queer sensation as if hands had *entered their body to do internal work*. Many of them said they felt the presence of *others* in the room.

Several years later, at a conference, I met the American clairvoyant healer Barbara Ann Brennan and bought her comprehensive book on healing, *Hands of Light*. Within its pages I found descriptions very similar to my own experiences and in-depth explanations that confirmed my own understanding.

Early on in my healing work, I had an interesting experience that left me toying with the idea that time is *spherical* not linear. Unlike linear time that flows in one direction - from the past towards the future - I became convinced that time moves in all directions, inwards, outwards, through the middle and out the other side. In meditation, I experienced time as consciousness, simultaneously travelling within and radiating out from me, paradoxically creating an experience of timelessness. Perhaps the idea that all time is simultaneous and multi-dimensional comes closest in description - but I am unable to articulate further.

The experience of seeing *spherical time* prompted me to look further into the subject of the *Universal Energy Field* that connects all of us. For the first time I became aware of quantum physics. My understanding of healing possibilities was altered forever as a consequence. I already knew that healing is not dependant on the person being present. Now I believed it possible to heal the past from the present and also the future. I saw the possibility of simultaneous healing not only for the client but also for their families and the situations surrounding them too, bringing everything back into alignment and radically altering of their reality. This idea increased my interest in the benefits and practice of distant healing.

In writing this I am aware there is another paradox. Though I have this understanding, I continue to operate and think in linear terms for the purposes of daily living and for the writing of this book.

These fascinating insights did not equip me to handle the toughest challenge of my healing career – *the dark night of the soul*. I had been healing for thirteen years when I left my marriage and fell into depression. The grief and despair lasted years. I felt abandoned by God and very angry. I lost my faith, my trust and confidence, doubting everything I had believed so implicitly before.

Becoming aware of how little I actually knew, I took a tumble down the *Jacob's Ladder* of spiritual certitude. It was a lonely, humbling rite of passage that put to the test all that I had accepted so easily beforehand. I emerged from it stronger, more resilient, more sensitive and compassionate towards other people facing their own challenging *dark nights of the soul*. Many left my clinic, aware of being on a voyage of discovery about themselves. Any sense of failure was seen as a challenge to be overcome and moved beyond. I was satisfied when that happened. Ultimately, that is what being an effective healer is all about – the facilitation of others to heal themselves and grow in understanding.

Time passed and there were more difficult periods. From each I emerged a bit wiser and more down to earth. I trained further in complementary therapies until I could offer an extensive, multi-disciplinary approach to my clients. And, while the practice grew, my understanding and vision was expanding. I began to see the possibilities of distance healing not just for people, but also for situations and the natural world. More and more it felt like my work needed to embrace the bigger picture - World Healing.

Before I can go any further with that, however, I need to backtrack and look more closely at some of the other footsteps that led me there.

ENTER THE NUMINOUS

'Until we accept the fact that life itself is founded in
mystery, we shall learn nothing.'
Henry Miller
'What lies behind us and what lies before us are tiny
matters, compared to what lies within us.'
Ralph Waldo Emerson
'I shut my eyes in order to see.'
Paul Gauguin

For many people, psychic experiences and phenomena
are questionable, even ridiculous. Some people find the idea
of exploring other realms through extra-sensory abilities
scary, even verging on witchcraft.

They once fascinated me, but now I confess that psychic
fayres and evenings of clairvoyance pose no attraction.
Workshops and ceremonies for spiritual ascension have the
same effect. The nearby town of Glastonbury, considered
by many *New Agers* to be *The Heart Centre* of the world,
has seen so many ceremonies conducted in and around it
opening portals into other realms, it must have an energy
field leakier than a tea bag! The welter of *how to* books
on psychic development and metaphysical knowledge

cramming shelves in *New Age* bookshops pass me by. I am cautious about channelled information on the future of humanity that stream through mediums who claim to be a channel for this or that ascended master. Maybe I am being unfairly dismissive, but years of experience in the field have made me more discerning. I consider 'I've been there, done that and got the T-shirt' for the most part - but perhaps that's arrogance.

Yet in spite of what I have just written, I have had many intriguing metaphysical moments. I am a down-to-earth Taurean, not flaky by nature, but the following experience could only be described as bizarre. It was one of the rare occasions when I saw my father really angry.

I could have been no more than eight and I was being rude. It was suppertime when formal table manners were observed but I ignored this and argued loudly about the withdrawal of my pocket money for an earlier misdemeanour. Finally I went too far. In a thunderous voice, my father sent me to my room until I mended my manners. I stormed into my room, stamping my feet hard on the polished brick floor in my anger and flung myself down on the bed.

It was not fair! My parents were stupid and cruel! Thoughts ran on and on, childish, unreasonable. They would be sorry! I would run away and find a family who appreciated me. I pictured myself enfolded in the loving arms of a handsome, sporty father and a perfect 'Vogue' housewife mother. That's what I deserved! I sat up again and, in a staccato wave of frustration, drummed a hard tattoo with my feet on the floor.

Something made me look up suddenly. The glass globe lampshade in the centre of the ceiling, fixed there in an optimistic hope that some day we would have electricity, was slowly unscrewing itself! I was overcome by a weird, detached wonder. Why was the lamp doing that? I don't remember being frightened, only dreamy as I watched the slow rotation. Everything seemed to be moving in slow motion.

Finally the globe detached itself, hung suspended for a long moment, then fell, smashing upon the floor. It exploded on impact into hundreds of pieces, startling me out of this strange state. I sat bewildered, watching the fragments of white glass spinning across the floor. Almost at once my father burst into the room and saw the mess on the floor.

'You naughty, naughty girl!' he shouted.

I protested that I was innocent but that only made him angrier. He bent me over his knee and gave me a hard spanking. Face down across his lap I looked at the fragments in puzzled astonishment, oblivious to the stinging slaps. My bewilderment did much to block out the pain of punishment. I never tried to explain what had happened, knowing that it would not be believed. I could hardly believe it myself.

Episodes of the spookier kind were not a common part of my childhood experience but, as a young child of six or seven, I was unnerved by a strange occurrence that happened regularly as I was falling asleep. I would hear an insistent stream of sound inside my head, growing steadily louder and more intense - a whining, drilling sound. With it came a sensation in my mouth as if words had been planted there that began to swell until it felt as if my mouth could no longer contain them. It was a horrible, nightmarish sensation that made my heart pound in panic. Each time it happened I jerked into full wakefulness and called out to my parents. I was so afraid of the strange sensation that I had years of difficulty going to sleep. Then suddenly it stopped and I forgot about it.

Only once since then have I had a repeat experience. It occurred in the late-1970s soon after we began practising deep relaxation in the development group. At home, tired from a day's teaching, I relaxed in a comfortable armchair with my eyes closed. My husband sat across from me, absorbed in a newspaper article – a scene of normal domesticity.

All at once a droning whine began like a giant mosquito

trapped inside my head and I felt a powerful force present. Suddenly that old, familiar sensation of the word growing in my mouth began. In a surge of panic, I leapt to my feet, rushed into the kitchen and immersed myself in a lot of energetic activity until the sensation had fully subsided. I was soaked in sweat from the experience. It was a long time before my pounding heart quietened.

Discussing it later with the psychic development teacher, it was concluded that I had sunk into a deep state of relaxation and had started going into trance. All at once my childhood experiences made sense to me. I may have always been susceptible to trance states and, not understanding the unfamiliar sensations, it was natural to find them frightening. Still, even with the new understanding, I was thoroughly put off the idea of surrendering control of myself - even to a wiser being! On my teacher's advice, the next time I sat down to practise meditation I sent out a silent message that I did not wish to serve as a trance medium. This request must have been received for that unnerving experience has never been repeated.

Instead, I developed a way to communicate with other levels without having to go into trance. If I sat in silence and wrote down, without questioning, whatever words dropped into my mind, profound and beautiful passages would eventually emerge. I sat at the same time each day, keeping my focus on just the word I was writing. I liken it to the telegraph ticker-tape messages of the past being tapped out one letter at a time. Only when I sensed that nothing else would come, did I read it back to myself. At the start there were strings of nonsense words but then simple, often beautiful sayings started to appear.

The first said this.

- *Fools are like dogs. When one starts to speak, others join in and those who hear close their ears and turn away. The wise man is like a cricket. He waits for the silence then starts to sing and all who hear stop to listen.*

I began to look forward to what came pouring through my pen. Much of it was counsel for myself, commenting on my perceptions and attitudes, and about how I lived my life.

- *The major way to conquer fear is to make a decision!* I was counselled this in a moment of fear and indecision. I taped this pithy bit of advice to the wall above the sink in the bathroom to catch my eye every time I entered. It steered me through a dark phase of my life at the time and continues to this day to be one of my favourite maxims.

So what was the origin of these messages? I called the source of this counsel *My Guide.* It was like having a personal advisor and teacher always present. It answered my questions simply and in words suited to my level of understanding at the time. The following are early examples of these dialogues.

'What do you mean by freedom?' I asked. My guide replied.

- *Of what? Freedom of will? Of choice of expression? Of movement? These are all ways in which most people think in terms of freedom. Remember this. You are always free inside yourself. No-one can restrict that freedom except you. <u>You</u> are the greatest tyrant to your own freedom. <u>You</u> are the most restricting of jailors.*

How true! All the same, it did not prevent me being imprisoned periodically in my own misperceptions and attitudes. Aware of this tendency, I asked the following question, 'Can you tell me how to release my limiting ideas?'

A sense of great peace descended over me as finer, faster energy flowed in.

- *I know how difficult it is for you to understand how you limit yourself. You have always been afraid of being wrong. This is your first, greatest and most fundamental limitation. If you get caught in the trap of anxiety about whether you have made a right or wrong choice, just step back and laugh and remember this is all a game. Like a dance, the steps can be changed again and again.*

'What is my sense of exhaustion all about?' I asked on another occasion.

- It is caused by parts of your own nature that are at war with each other. Listen more closely to what each has to say and resolve the conflict.

Once it had been spelt out, it was obvious. There were conflicting emotions surrounding my job and these were the source of much stress. Straightaway it felt easier to resolve the particular issues involved. Maybe I would have eventually understood this for myself without the aid of a guide, but having root causes clearly presented like this speeded up the resolution. It also cut down the possibilities for any self-deception.

As time passed, I came to believe that whoever was answering was in fact an aspect of myself – albeit a wiser perspective. In some spiritual traditions this is known as the *Higher Self*. I began to think of it as my *Inner Wise Being*, always on hand and ready to communicate with me. Through it I was able to access levels beyond my normal level of understanding. The subjects covered became more complex. I was intrigued about imagination and asked, 'Where do ideas come from?' The *Inner Wise Being* replied.

- An idea is a process in which the Self is involved. It (the Self) stretches beyond physical confines to reach into pools of knowledge. This fund (of knowledge) is common to all beings. You all have the same 'resources room' from which to draw.

- The conscious personality controls the thought processes. All ideas originate from Truth, (which springs) from the Source, but it is not often they arrive in their purest form. Most often they are distorted, warped by the filters of the conscious personality.

- The Source is made up of all sides – positive and negative. A negative, destructive personality draws on the negative resources in the

common pool of knowledge. When negative elements group together without positive counterbalances, evil is the result. Nothing but positive elements without their negative counterbalances can be just as harmful.

Although not exactly answering my question, I had been given enough to chew on, particularly about negative and positive attitudes. It prompted me to enquire about a series of negative experiences I was going through at the time. The *Inner Wise Being* flowing through my pen had this to say.

- It seems you still feel a need to explore and experience the cause and effect of choice. At present you are exploring the effects resulting from choices of weakness rather than strength. What you are currently experiencing will continue until you no longer feel the need to do so.

'But wrong choices can cause great pain and frustration and, in my case, exhaustion!' I protested.

- Your life is a continuous journey towards developing wisdom and discernment. You learn through having your own way and falling into situations of your own making. The feelings of frustration and pain are gifts pushing you to learn how to make appropriate choices that change the pattern of the future for the better.

This comment helped me see how weak choices ultimately made me feel dissatisfied, defensive, disempowered - even my body expressed a sense of weakness as a result - whereas choices made from strength made me feel positive and energized. The upshot of this was that I felt stimulated, alive, and my brain seemed to work better. This motivated me to make choices with greater awareness, and the negative episode came quickly to an end.

There was a downside, however, to receiving information and knowledge in this way. I began to have difficulty concentrating on the written word. I would buy books to learn more but found I could not focus on the content beyond a passage, or maybe a chapter, that confirmed or expanded what had arrived through my internal messaging service.

Or I might get the solution to a crisis.

On one occasion when contemplating a new venture, I badly needed some encouragement. I happened to visit *Waterstones*, the bookshop, and, while browsing along the bookshelves, a book fell on my head. Startled, I picked up *Feel the Fear and Do It Anyway* by Susan Jeffers. I registered the message and went ahead with my new venture with a confidence born in that moment. Experiences like this are often reported. They appear to be commonplace when there is some kind of crisis.

Books that I bought in the optimistic hope that I would

read them were given away. At first I was defensive and felt there was something wrong with me - erudite people surrounded me, quoted from fascinating books offering keys to spiritual attainment. Then it dawned on me that I was gaining information in a unique way and that, as soon as I understood it, I was given external confirmation of its correctness. I was learning and integrating knowledge in a compact way. Nothing was diluted through being scattered. There were no diversions, no digressing. No intellectualizing.

I still find it hard to read serious books. I joke about it, saying my reading muscles have become flabby, but I quietly hope that one day I will be able to wade through a *heavyweight* book with ease.

A FORK IN THE ROAD

A NEW DIRECTION BEGINS

'To know that what is impenetrable to us really exists, manifesting itself as the highest wisdom and the most radiant beauty...'
Albert Einstein
'God must become an activity in our consciousness.'
Joel S. Goldsmith
'Man can learn nothing except by going from the known to the unknown.'
Claude Bernard

It was in the early 1980s that I began to *hear* a voice. This was not my *Inner Wise Being*. It came from a different source, a profound and dramatic departure from the *ticker-tape dictation* to which I had become accustomed to.

Many people from differing backgrounds and different religious persuasions have experienced *hearing* a voice and many have interpreted the powerful feeling as God speaking to them through their souls. All have reported the sense of a numinous presence - of being surrounded by a loving and infinitely wise influence. Certainly my own experience has always been one of a great sense of security whenever the voice spoke to me.

- *Manifest your dreams through the state of gratitude*, the voice said simply one day. I was leaning back against a large beech tree in the local park at the time, devising ways of raising money so that I could attend a healing conference.

- Gratitude is the most earthing of states to be in. It connects you to the Earth in a state of profound love. It is an important healing state both for the Earth and for you. You cannot manifest your dreams in the flowing way possible when you are un-earthed.

I have never forgotten this simple piece of advice. It has become another of the guiding principles of my life.

The information I received over the years through this form of guidance has been a great source of knowledge and advice. Unfolding events have shown again and again that what I am told is accurate. The trouble is I often misinterpreted what was said at the time because of my tendency to leap to conclusions. In spite of myself, events have always steered my footsteps in the direction I need to go, with my understanding stumbling along in the rear as shown in the following story.

It was the summer of 1997. I sat quietly and focused on the trip I was about to make to the World Healing Conference in California. I was excited knowing that it was a time of great opportunity.

I closed my eyes and, after a while, became aware that I was receiving a strong impression about what the journey would mean for me. It was as if the silence itself was speaking, flowing into my consciousness on a wavelength of silver. I knew this 'Silver Voice'. For years, it had 'spoken' to me and guided me at important times.

It delivered an intriguing message. During my time in the USA, I was going to find three places of power. There I would become 'earthed' in a new and powerful way. This would form my 'bridge to the sky'.

What did that mean? I wondered.

The Silver Voice elaborated. It would enable me to manifest my dreams more easily and potently.

I was told of a place of power by the sea. I figured this would probably be Monterey, where the conference was to be held. I would find a second place in the mountains, the 'Voice' continued. As I intended to visit the Yosemite National Park, I took it for granted I would find it there. Suddenly the word 'Esselen' popped into my head, accompanied by an image of me soaking in hot bubbling water under a full moon sailing across a starry sky. This would be a third place of power. Hearing the word but not seeing the spelling, I assumed this to be the Esalen Institute for self-growth, situated on the old coastal road south of Monterey. There were natural hot springs an outsider could visit between midnight and three a.m. So a trip to the Institute during the time of the full moon became part of my plans, as an absolute 'must do'.

How wrong I was in most of my assumptions! Everything took place exactly as the voice described but, apart from being right about Monterey, nothing else was as I had imagined it to be and they turned out to be far more profound.

The Monterey Beach Hotel, where the conference was held, was situated in a spectacular water's-edge position. Tired after the journey, I decided to miss the opening presentations and stayed on the beach instead. Through making this decision, the first part of the prophecy came to pass.

Sitting on the sand, in contact with the four elements – earth, air, fire and water - I visualised a source of Power and Light above my head. I breathed it in through the crown of my head and out through the soles of my feet into the Earth. It was an exercise I had done many times before, but this time the effect was different from anything I had ever felt before.

There was a tremendous surge of energy and an explosion of colour filled my vision. I found myself seeing everything in magenta - sand, sea, sky and people. My vision cleared and I saw a rainbow instead: vivid red, intense orange and deep yellow, followed by softer, subtle greens, blue-greens, blues and violets. The coloured arc was breathtaking and, significantly, the colours were reversed. Instantly, I knew my 'bridge to the sky' had been formed.

The summit came to an end and I accepted an invitation to stay with another healer in North California. Just as we set off she astonished me by announcing that we would not be going straight to her home. We had been invited to take part in a Bear Clan ceremony nearby. The invitation had come from Tom Little Bear, the tribal head of the Esselen people.

'You won't mind the detour, will you?' she said anxiously, misinterpreting my expression.

Esselen! In that instant, I knew that the Silver Voice had been referring to this Native American tribe, not the Esalen Institute. Their tribal grounds cover a large area in the Ventana Wilderness, a mountainous area flanking the Big Sur region of California. Now, for the first time in their history, the Esselen were hosting a gathering of Bear Clans - due to start that afternoon after the healing summit ended in Monterey!

And so, the second part of my prophetic message began to unfold.

The unpaved road wound up into the mountain wilderness, through steep-sided mountain passes. Pines with roots anchored amongst rocks eighty feet below, soared up into the sky, at times blocking our view. Overhead, a lone eagle tracked our progress up the long, dusty road to our destination. Tom Little Bear met us and led us in a solemn

procession to the meeting place. One by one we entered a small opening and, crouching almost double, filed along a passage shaped like a birth canal that opened into a cavernous space, half buried in the earth.

We were inside the ceremonial roundhouse of the Bear Clans. Light filtered through the smoke from a hole in the roof above the central fire pit. Four large timbers, one at each point of the compass, supported the roof. In the gloom I saw that we outnumbered the Bear Clan members and I realised the majority had yet to arrive.

Speaking in measured tones, Tom Little Bear opened the ceremony by telling us the story of The Great Medicine Wheel. He paced around the central fire, stopping at each point of the compass in turn. He spoke of the history and visions of his people and the purpose of the Bear Clans' gathering.

All the while, a drum beat out a steady rhythm. The power built and throbbed in the air as the dust motes glittered in the shafts of sunlight, and the smoke swirled through the hole in the roof.

Tom Little Bear pulled out a cloth-wrapped object. He unwrapped it, revealing at last the talking stick of his tribe. He pointed to the black crow feathers bound to it at one end. When people sit in council, he said, each person who speaks is required to hold the talking stick and speak with integrity.

'These feathers are there to remind you to speak truly. They are there acting as witness to the truth of your statements. It is a sacred moment.' Holding the stick firmly in both hands, he bade each healer in turn to make a statement of intention regarding our own part in world service.

Seventy people voiced their vision and their commitment in that sacred space, passing the talking stick from one to another. With each statement the energy around us rose and gained power. I reached for the stick, my heart pounding as loudly as the drum. I might fail!

Grasping the stick tightly, I made a commitment to do all in my power to safeguard life on earth. A surge of deep love and respect for

the Earth Mother moved through me. I savoured my newly awakened passion and knew this was a commitment that would last the rest of my life.

The ceremony ended. We emerged from the roundhouse into the deep shadows of late afternoon. It was getting late - too late for most people to start their long trip homewards. I was invited to stay overnight at the home of one of the conference contributors who lived on the edge of the tribal grounds. A short while later, I stood gazing up at the wooden building nestling amongst trees on the steep hillside, glad that I could prolong the powerful experience by staying a while longer in the area.

A striking, big-boned woman with silver-blond hair came out on the wooden deck to greet me. Behind her padded three large dogs, one of which was pure white. These were not dogs but wolves! They peered through the wooden bars, necks craning, tongues lolling, their gazes deeply penetrating.

My hostess held open the fly-screen door and gestured for me to enter. Inside were other conference members busy preparing a meal. The evening passed and, one by one, people drifted away to their beds until only four of us were left talking quietly over cups of coffee. Midnight was approaching. I left the others and made my way to the outdoor hot-tub situated higher up the hillside. Two misty figures were half hidden in the steam, another conference member and a traditional storyteller for the Cherokee Nation.

At times talking, at times quiet, we relaxed together. Midnight passed. My conference companion and I fell silent, listening to wisdom stories. Comprehension grew in me about the power of story for imparting deeper truths and conveying concepts that are difficult to grasp. Our psyches and cultures are filled with narratives, or stories, which influence our awareness and behaviour.

Later, snuggled in a sleeping bag, I fell asleep thinking of hot bubbling water under the full moon and the stars. The last part of my prophetic vision had happened exactly as foretold.

Storytelling has become more important to me through subsequent years as an outcome of that meeting. I find it a powerful way of introducing new concepts and encouraging individuals to entertain different possibilities. Recognizing that it is possible to challenge perceptions through story and anecdote without being too confrontational, I have begun considering how story metaphor can be used to inspire change on a much larger magnitude.

But stories get broken too. You can wander off the point and lose the plot, and this has happened in my life story more than once.

I am not alone in believing that we are born with a life-purpose, whether it is to be a business-person, a communicator, a leader, a healer or an artist. We feel contentment and fulfilment when we are a playing our role in the correct story. When, as sadly often happens, we find ourselves in work that is not ours to do, we feel profoundly dissatisfied, frustrated and depressed. This happens frequently within our culture where great value is placed on monetary wealth and being seen to be successful. For some this sad state continues throughout their lives, but others reach a critical point and are galvanized into a change of direction.

There have been two major periods when I felt I lost my way, becoming disconnected from my Self. These were times of angry frustration and shame, feeling isolated and insecure. One was after my marriage breakdown and the second was following an accident in Australia (I'll come to that later). Unable to tap into intuition, I had had to rely on my conscious mind and reason. I was unable to appreciate how both of these periods played an extremely valuable part in my personal development.

There are two sayings, 'Everything happens for a purpose'

and 'Everything happens as it should'. There was both purpose and benefit in having breaks from inner guidance, which reminds me of another saying - 'If you don't use it you lose it'. I began to use the wonderful and unique tool I have at my disposal, my brain. My memory needed exercise and discipline like the rest of my body. If I wanted to be able to inspire, be a motivator in these times of change, it would be an advantage to remember statistics, the facts and figures of events, not just to rely on visionary insights and a cosmic overview.

I set to work exercising my mental faculties for information gathering and recollection. First I joined a choir, learning complex musical structures and singing songs from memory, then went on to acquire complicated new skills with the unfamiliar technology of a quantum, biofeedback healing-tool called the SCIO. It's a revolutionary appliance created by Professor Bill Nelson, which took many years of research and development to combine holistic medicine with advanced quantum technology. Using the SCIO expanded my understanding about simultaneity in time and how everything interconnects. Intellectually I was stretched to the limits of my comprehension.

During trainings, I rubbed shoulders with therapists who ran health clinics, coming to appreciate the skills used in the business world even if I was out of sympathy with much of the ethos. These people were articulate and practical decision-makers, practised in assertiveness and communication. Well versed in negotiating, they knew how to project themselves in a positive way. They were efficient timekeepers and good at collating and summarising information - skills sharply honed and practised with ease.

Surrounded by all this intellectual stimulation, my inner guidance became even less active. The feelings that I had lost my way rose to the surface again. But I hadn't

- this turned out to be a valuable revision period. Having to rely on memory and reason more than on intuition for a time, exercised my rational powers and made me appreciate the facet of wisdom that others, without my gifts, have to rely upon - good common sense. Common sense is the counterpart to the more fey qualities of instinct, intuition and inner directives. All are needed for balanced development.

I was recently reminded of something I have long believed. There is no order or time limit on personal growth. Life is not a race. We learn things when we are ready for them and not before. Some years ago, after berating myself for being a failure and for not being cleverer or wiser, my *Inner Wise Being* chided me gently.

-You have been chosen by me as the most perfect vehicle for my purpose on Earth at this time. What is good enough for me should be good enough for you!

I was then shown that the way our soul evolves is similar to how a sea anemone feeds itself. Its tentacles are never all extended at the same time. Some gather information and food while others relax. Only when what has been collected is drawn back to be absorbed by the organism do other tentacles extend to collect something different. Similarly, as incarnated spiritual beings, we could never learn everything at once. That would be both overwhelming and indigestible.

Taking that into consideration, perhaps the most valuable aspect of seemingly losing my way is the time it gave me to absorb experiences, deepen my understanding and reach new levels of maturity. What I had learned could be taken back out into the world.

THE STONE SPIRAL – ALERT TO SYNCHRONICITY

'Growth is a spiral process, doubling back on itself,
reassessing and regrouping.'
Julia Margaret Cameron

'This seems to be the law of progress in everything we do; it moves
along a spiral rather than a perpendicular; we seem to be actually
going out of the way, and yet it turns out that we were
really moving upward all the time.'
Frances E. Willard

I view the events of my life as cyclical in nature. Or, to be more accurate, it seems that I am travelling through life in a spiral, arriving at an experience similar to one I have met before but at a level that offers a wider perspective of past events. Sometimes it reinforces and enriches what I have already learned but often it gives me another chance to comprehend something that I have not previously understood.

The compassionate universe we live in gives us repeated opportunities to become aware of hitherto unrecognized aspects of ourselves. New situations arrive highlighting old repeating patterns, limiting perceptions and assumptions.

Shortly after writing the book *Quest for Unity*, I went through an oft-repeated pattern highlighting my lack of trust when nothing appears to be happening in my life. Even though I am aware that intense activity is frequently followed by a lull, I imagined I had done something wrong. I sank into frustrated depression. Then in the cyclical nature of things, there began to be more movement in my life again. I went to Gambia with a charity and there, unexpectedly, I received a stone gift, one of many I have been given over the years. It was an occasion surrounded by synchronicity.

I lurched forward in my seat as the wheels hit the runway and the engines roared in reverse slowing the plane to taxiing speed. Through the porthole window the sun bounced off the whitewashed terminal building in a blinding glare.

Gambia!

As we taxied to a standstill, I reflected on events earlier in the day. I had had a couple of hours to kill before I left home for the airport. The house was in moderate order so I had used the time for meditation. I stared down at the flickering flame of the scented candle and attempted to quieten my busy thoughts. I was excited about the trip and with a quiet period in my life ending this seemed a good moment to seek guidance. I asked for a sign to guide my footsteps in the following year. Satisfied with my request, I packed everything away and left for the airport.

Within an hour of arriving at the Holiday Beach Club Hotel in Kololi, my sister and I were on the beach feeling rather put out by an unusually chilly breeze that whipped up the sand and made us glad of the cardigans around our shoulders.

Despite the breeze, the sun shone and the beach felt warm beneath my feet. I removed my sandals and dug my toes into the soft dry sand feeling the gritty grains shifting, working their way between my toes. The sea looked beautiful, the rhythmic sound of the waves finding an echo of response within me. It conjured up past memories of a beach in California when I had walked on soft sand in similar conditions.

Like then, I was surrounded by the four elements: Earth, Air, Fire and Water.

As I followed the ebb and flow of the surf-line, I silently repeated my request for a sign or message. Almost at once, I stubbed my toe against a small stone, dislodging it from the sand.

How disappointing!

If this was my sign, it did not look at all inspiring. True, it was circular and that symbolized an ongoing theme in my life of 'coming into wholeness', as I describe it, but, oh, it looked so uninspiringly dull, a plain flat stone with a roughened surface of a nondescript, sandy colour. I picked it up, chiding myself for wanting and expecting something more dramatic, more spectacular, to appear.

Once laid in my palm, however, I became aware of the sensation of sharp ridges on the hidden surface. I flipped it over. Revealed was a beautiful, perfect spiral, winding tightly into the middle.

I traced the ridged form into the middle and then found that I could return to the outer edge by following the trough – it was a double spiral. Spirals are meaningful to me symbolizing the Universe, the All-Powerful Unifying Force underlying creation.

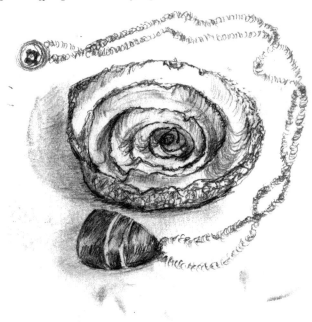

For indigenous people they're sacred, representing the continuous, eternal rhythm and natural direction of life. Carved by our ancestors in stone and wood, spirals can be seen depicting the cosmic dance of life, death, re-birth at sacred sites all over Britain and around the world. A powerful message indeed! My attitude was transformed. Now I was flooded with excitement at this auspicious find. I had been given my focus and direction for the coming year.

I continued walking, hugging the enormity of my find to myself, responding to my sister's chatter with appropriate noises while thinking of possible meanings for me. After a while she challenged me about my absentminded responses. I showed her the stone. With our heads bent over the spiral stone we failed to notice the arrival of a large group of young Gambian men until we were surrounded.

Wide smiles split their faces.

'How are you?'

'Where do you come from?'

'What's your name?'

Persistent, pushy, questions bubbling up constantly. They crowded close, friendly, meaning no offence, unconscious of boundaries both physical and social. The pressure of their friendliness was overwhelming. We responded politely while trying to create some space for ourselves, but memories of the Apartheid rose on a wave of shame. I wanted to atone for the white arrogance and indifference I had seen as a child in South Africa. The injustice in the wealth-gap separating us. These boys had so little. In their eyes I must have seemed incredibly rich. I wanted to respond with more warmth but in that moment what I needed was privacy and time to acclimatize.

No, we did not want to go on a tour of their village now. Later, perhaps. No, we couldn't say when. No, we were not going to be there for more than three days. We were part of a charity delivering bicycles to schools.

Finally I said, 'It's very nice to meet all of you but now we're tired and want to be by ourselves.' Typically British!

It did not work. We tried to make an escape by walking back towards the hotel steps. At this point one of the youths, wearing a bright yellow T-shirt with the word 'Yosemite' across the chest, reached up to his neck, unclasped a necklace and placed it round my neck.

'You are my special friend. Please help me. Will you sponsor my education.'

I thanked him for the necklace, making some lame excuse about many financial commitments. Said goodbye.

Back in the hotel room, I admired the necklace in the mirror. Handmade and beautiful. Small beads strung on fishing line on either side of a larger triangular shaped glass bead - black with two bands of white slashed across its surface. The necklace, clasped together by a press-stud, fitted snugly round my neck. Somehow it felt special, with a greater significance than I could put my finger on in the moment. Was there a link between this gift and the spiral stone I had found earlier?

Again, I felt ashamed at how I had reacted to the young men. In true British style I had fobbed them off with empty promises. They may have been bumpsters, a derogatory Gambian name for groups of unemployed youths who hassle the tourists, but how I wished I had given 'Yosemite' a reciprocal gift.

Next day my sister supplied the connection in an idle moment of conversation. The black pendant bead signified the Gambian symbol for Unity - that word again! It all made perfect sense, in the context of spiral symbolism and my endeavour for wholeness. The theme for the year was about being aware of the rhythms and cycles, the flow of unifying energy connecting everything in my life. The necklace just reinforced it.

On my return to England, I showed a close friend the spiral stone and the necklace, recounting how I had come by them. What significance they had for me. I talked about the bumpsters and of my regret.

The conversation then turned to the progress of her writing and the book she was reading. 'It is such an intriguing book,' she said. 'You must read it after I have finished.'

She rang me up later that day. 'You wont believe this but your story about the bumpsters in Gambia – I have just come across it again in that book!'

'What do you mean?'

'The book is about a young woman who goes to Gambia and, while walking on the beach, is beset by a group of young men. One places a necklace around her neck. Extraordinary coincidence, don't you think?'
I had to agree.

A couple of weeks later, I read the book myself – 'Sleeping in the Sand' by Crysse Morrison - and found many parallels with my own life.

It was all about searching for, and finding, lost fragments of a young woman's life. In the story, everything moves towards a meeting in a Gambian marketplace between the woman and a twin she did not know she had, the missing piece of herself of which she had always been instinctively aware. Reading it when I did felt like a postscript to the trip, a reinforcement of the message in the stone spiral.

Happenings such as this abound in my life. At a Healing Summit in California, eight years earlier, I had encountered a different sort of spiral on a beach - a labyrinth. On that occasion I had shuffled hand-in-hand with others, part of a human chain of intention, walking out of the old world and into the new. That ceremony had marked a new phase in my life too. One also marked by meaningful coincidences.

I see synchronicity as an unusual occurrence, a collision of events so outside the box of normal experience it grabs our attention. On the threshold of imminent change, I am often more aware of synchronous happenings. In common with others, I view their appearance as signs, confirmation for choices made or for insights being correct. Like neon lights pointing the way, they have led me on quests both physical and spiritual, not all of them comfortable, but all inviting learning, as the following anecdote illustrates.

Not long ago, I went for a healing session with a friend who has trained in several shamanic traditions, including those of Central America, Cuba and Africa. His healing room in Bath is an unusual, beautiful space below ground level. It has a womb-like feel and a deeply nurturing atmosphere. Even in the soft, dimmed light the earthy colours of the fabrics were richly vibrant.

The shaman invited me on a journey to contact Grandfather Fire; the dawn air was crisp, cold and the warm flames were comforting. Then the soft, rhythmic drumbeat carried me to a place where birds were singing and there was a smell of lavender in the air. The sound of a stream. The shaman's voice in the distance inviting me to reconnect with my dreams and hopes for the future.

I thought of my desire for companionship, for sharing and support, for freedom from burdens. A list of longings followed, for beauty, reverence, awe, wonder, respect, love, a sense of harmony. For my feet to be guided on the path to these experiences. They slipped into pale cream doeskin moccasins decorated with little silver fish charms. Both moccasins and decorations felt symbolically significant of courage and determination to follow my way home to The Source. All the while, as if from a vast distance, I could hear the shaman chant and shake his rattle.

I focused on Grandfather Fire again. I was hungry and scooped up a flame and ate it. It had substance - like food. I swallowed it and felt it in my stomach. It felt so good. I looked down and could see it – fire in the belly! Wow, I thought.

I sat in the car after the session and wrote down my experience, still feeling the influence of Grandfather's warmth, and seeing vivid, dancing colour. As I started writing the description of how I had eaten fire, two tortoiseshell butterflies flew in through the open car window chasing each other in a spiral dance. Their flame-coloured wings brushed against my face and then both were gone again. Magic!

On other occasions, strange events have come in response to a request for a sign or to confirm a dream message, as happened in the following encounter.

A few early golfers teed off in the distance. For a brief moment the sun shone through lighting the edges of the encircling cloud with shimmering golden-white light before the gap closed once more like the lens-eye of a camera.

Breathing in the fragrance of the newly mown grass on the first fairway, I wound in and out of the pine trees. They stood as silent sentinels flanking the edge, their roots hidden in the longer grass.

While scanning the grass for early field mushrooms, I spotted a brown mound that looked out of place in the surroundings. The back of a young hare! It crouched there with its eyes closed to slits, ears laid flat along its back. Was it frozen in fear and playing dead? I withdrew slightly to give it the chance of escape but it remained still. Concerned then that it might be injured, I looked more closely whereupon the creature stood up, stretched its limbs and yawned widely. After a few steps away from me it dropped back into a crouch and nibbled grass within its reach. Perfectly at ease.

It was a unique situation. I was transfixed.

I moved forward cautiously but this time my movement made it take off in a blur of speed. It then did something curious, running in a circle to return within a few feet of me. It settled to grazing once more.

I stayed a while watching, marvelling at the strangeness, then continued my walk. Half an hour later, I returned to find the hare still there on exactly the same spot. Once again the hare took off at speed and, as before, circled back. It seemed unperturbed by my presence so I sat down and watched it.

It was significant that I should stumble across the hare on this day of all days. The night before, I had been in a group discussing totem animals within different shamanic traditions and religions. I wondered about my own totem (power) animal. Ask, was the advice from the group.

I did - that night I dreamt about a hare.

In Europe the hare has strong association with the Earth Mother and Eostre, the Anglo Saxon Moon Goddess who gave her name to Easter. In early Christian traditions of Britain, it is the Easter hare that lays the Easter egg that symbolizes the dawn of new life. As a result the hare has come to represent new beginnings, rebirth, resurrection and rejuvenation. I liked the idea of a hare being my totem animal, but I wanted further proof to be certain.

And here I was, with a hare that showed no intention of going! It was I who went leaving the small brown form peacefully feeding, a silhouette in the early morning light.

I had just met one of my totem animals.

Again I find myself contemplating the events surrounding the stone spiral. Was there more to my Gambian experience and Crysse Morrison's book than a coincidental link? I wonder. Was the return to Africa part of my life's journey for a particular moment of healing? Is it in Africa that I, too, have to find my lost pieces? I will have to wait for another turn of the spiral to have that answered. For now I have more questions than answers.

I feel the tug of Africa as I write, the land of my birth. For a brief moment I feel uprooted like a plant, unable to flourish so vigorously away from my native soil. Away from the smells, the tastes, the sounds. From that wonderful, instinctive rhythm. On African soil I could feel the heart-beat of the planet. I feel a real longing. Africa was not something I outgrew. I left because I had to, not because I wanted to.

THE AXE – THE CALL OF THE EARTH

'Take from the altars of the past the fire - not the ashes.'
Jean Jaures
*'What is the fire in our belly but the eternal flame
of a thousand ancestors.'*
Robert Brault
*'...Every great enterprise begins with and takes its
first forward step in faith.'*
Friedrich Schlegel
*'The challenge of history is to recover the past and
introduce it to the present.'*
David Thelen

As I waited for members of my healing circle to arrive, I moved the table altar to the centre of the room and re-arranged the objects so that they represented the shamanic tradition of four directions - North, South, East and West - with the corresponding elements of earth, air, fire and water. Sitting side by side on the table were the Neolithic hand-axe and a stone-finger - the witness stone - representing Earth.

I touched them both, remembering the day they had entered my life. How, while floundering ankle-deep in mud on Severn Beach near Bristol, I had struggled to keep my balance. Wryly, I smiled to myself and thought how often I have felt mired in self-doubt and confusion, struggling to find balance, wanting to give up, yet all the time with that niggling sense that what I wanted was there just out of reach.

That fateful day was a moment when Earth seemed to reach out and make contact. I had joined a shamanic group dedicated to resolving racial tensions in the city that many believe can be traced back to the injustices of the slave trade. What happened that day is, I consider, the most momentous event of my life.

I looked down at the mud and caught my breath.

Oh no! It couldn't be! I stared with horror at a grey finger thrusting out of the mud, pointing skywards. The fear was fleeting, dissolving swiftly, as I realized the finger was stone; a fluke of nature had created a digit with well-defined fingernail and wrinkled knuckles.

Up to this point, I had been following instructions of the shaman, Roy Little Sun. His words echoed back to me. Find one hundred and eight stones shaped like Africa to create a medicine wheel, he had instructed, adding the final words 'And find a special stone to mark the day for yourself'.

Picking my way carefully and sticking closely to the mud-line of the Severn Beach, I searched for stones against the backdrop of the old Severn Bridge. Its smudged blue outline stretched away through the haze across the mouth of the estuary. Beyond it was the coastline of Wales just discernable in the grey distance.

Close by me were twenty others doing the same. We were preparing for a ceremony to heal the 'African Wound' – a legacy of the slave trade, which rises as unrest from time to time in the area of St Paul's where Afro-Caribbean and other ethnic minorities live.

It was a cold, March morning - a far cry from the heat of my African childhood. The stagnant stench of waterlogged mud rose in sulphurous waves with every footstep, in stark contrast to the dry savannah landscape of the High Veldt with its clean scent of long dry grass and hot earth. I had thought it extremely unlikely to find many stones shaped like Africa on this beach, let alone a special one to mark the occasion.

But I was wrong. Here was a special stone.

I picked up the stone finger and examined carefully. But as I moved to put it in my pocket I 'heard' a 'voice' in my head clearly say,

- No! Follow the pointing finger. It will lead you to your special stone!

Shocked, I looked down at the finger lying in my hand. The finger was pointing out towards the tide line. It did not cross my mind to disobey so I started off across the mud. Before long I was ankle deep and struggling to keep both my balance and my shoes.

'This is ridiculous!' I thought. 'How stupid to follow instructions from a voice and a finger of stone!' I turned to go back.

- No, said the voice and repeated - Follow the pointing finger. It will lead you to your special stone.

Obediently, I walked out into the sea of mud. About two hundred metres farther on, and just as I was passing a curious lump of earth topped with sedge grass, the voice suddenly spoke again.

- STOP! Dig!

At my feet was a smooth mound of mud suggesting some object might be concealed beneath. It was impossible to discern its shape or know its size, but instinct told me that it was something important. I felt excited, rather than scared, by the strangeness of what was occurring.

My fingers probed into the glutinous mud, scooping it aside to release

what lay beneath. As I did so a parade of images floated through my mind; images of hunter-gatherer people living the way of their ancestors; African Bushmen crouched around their fire under the densely clustered stars of the African sky, their skins glowing orange from reflected flames. The scene dissolved and re-formed as Australian Aborigines. The figure of a man loomed in the foreground, a dark shape leaning on a throwing stick silhouetted against the night sky.

All this I registered as my fingers encountered something hard and smooth. I worked around the edges to release the object and lifted it clear, still covered by gobbets of mud. After washing it clean in a puddle, I examined it.

It was about eight inches long, made of stone, curved at one end and tapering to a blunt point at the other. A perfect, beautifully fashioned Neolithic ceremonial hand-axe at least six thousand years old (as identified by archaeologists of Bristol University). This was a special stone indeed and I was awed by the responsibility of finding it.

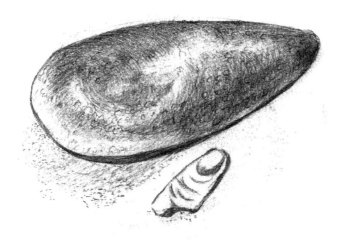

I recalled the hunter-gather images seen in my mind. They now seemed highly significant. In the summer I was going to Australia and I knew there would be an opportunity to meet Aboriginal people. Everything, I believed, suggested a link between the finding of the axe and the journey to Australia. Buoyed by this belief, the axe and its companion - the finger that pointed the way - accompanied me as I embarked upon an amazing adventure in search of a place and the people who lived there. I could never have imagined the events that were to follow, but that is another story. (That search is described in detail in my first book, *Quest For Unity*.)

On reflection, what took place that day mirrored the psychological journey through the rich and fertile mud of my life. On a microcosmic level of healing, I knew that the unhealed aspects of my past needed to come into the present for healing if I wanted to live a fulfilling future. But interest in self-growth work of this kind had begun to change. My focus was shifting, my horizons widening.

Awareness of the interconnection between everything kept being reinforced over the years. Again and again, I was thrown back into the childhood experience of knowing I was an integral part of the whole. Eventually, the implications of this dawned on me. Whatever I did for myself, I did for everything else. I began to look at the larger picture – the macrocosm of existence as well as the microcosm of the individual.

It opened my healing group to a new way of working. Gone was the focus on self, alone. Everything we now did was with the intention of bringing some benefit, however small, to the greater picture. The imbalances, the unresolved anger and pain, the sense of injustice and lack – we worked on all of them, using our own situations as proxy for the world. There was no way to avoid awareness of uncomfortable global issues - increasing disparity between rich and poor countries, a lack of balance in fair distribution of wealth and its benefits, exploitation of the planetary resources and damage to the environment. Healing, as a consequence, became more and more world-focused.

Following my adventures with the hand-axe, a cycle seemed to come to an end. I entered the doldrums. The axe lay quietly, wrapped in cloth, its part in my life dormant. Then, two years ago, a dream prompted me to remove it from its wrapping once more.

Turning it over in my hands, feeling its smoothness and weight, I had had a flash of insight about this beautiful object – something I had failed to register at the time. Something linked with the times and challenges we are currently experiencing.

A gift from the ancient world had been delivered into my hands - a message from Earth - about the need for the two worlds, ancient and modern, to come together for the survival of both; a harmonious integration of aboriginal awareness of belonging to the land, with the creative gifts and knowledge of the modern world.

The images I had seen of hunter-gatherer people, Bushmen and Australian Aborigines, supported this insight. World events seem to be pushing humanity - and Western culture in particular - towards finding a healthier, balanced and more fulfilling way of life. With the gift of the hand-axe, I was being shown a way forward. Coinciding with this insight, I was told that in Neolithic cosmology axes were seen to represent the feminine.

I heard this without surprise.

STONEKEEPER – FINDING BALANCE

'Remember, stone is the ancestor of all, is of the beginning and the timeless spirit that joins star to star and age to age.
Out of stone comes life.'
Song of the Circle, Barry Brailsford
'The consciousness of the planet is leading humanity to the re-discovery of an ancient and forgotten healing art in which the utilization of crystals is prominent.'
Melody

Before I go further, I need to explain something. I am born under the sign of Taurus. Taureans, in esoteric circles, are said to be Earth keepers. Whether that is true or not, I do feel I have a special relationship with the Earth, an intimate contact that keeps intervening in my life and bringing about change.

Over the past fifteen years I have had several extraordinary experiences - other than finding the axe-head and spiral - which are directly linked with stones and crystals. In common with large numbers of people, I find stones and crystals beautiful and fascinating. There is evidence supporting the belief that they emit different frequencies of energy, some of which can be used to heal and assist us in our personal development.

My first significant encounter with crystals happened during a counsellor training in Weston-super-Mare. I was about to confront one of the tutors over a bit of unpleasantness and I was very nervous, dreading the meeting. I ducked back into the car to collect my bag and was surprised by a sudden sparkle of light flashing on the driver's seat. A tiny quartz crystal smaller than anything I possessed lay sparkling on the fabric. Its peculiar brilliance seemed to emanate strength. Instantly I felt reassured that everything would go well for me. It did.

Following this, I had several experiences where I received insights that seemed to spring directly from the consciousness of the planet. The most unusual of these occurred in Northern Spain.

I was out walking one morning with a companion, who had settled in Spain, enjoying the wonderful clarity of early morning Mediterranean light. In the distance, I spotted a sandy red scar in the hillside, showing the telltale signs of excavation. My companion, knowing I was interested in crystals, said stones with white quartz deposits could be found there. We descended along an uneven, boulder-strewn path, sidestepping down the final slope onto a flat area of rich, orange-red soil. I became aware of feeling disquiet. Something was wrong, I enquired about it.

'They are going to cover the hillside with holiday homes. It could be that,' my companion suggested.

'That's not good! Something must be done to protect this land!' I exclaimed. A glint of light from the ground in front of me caught my attention. It was so bright that I bent down to see what it was. To my astonishment, it was a perfect tiny *double-terminated wand* (a faceted crystal shaped like a wand which is pointed at each end) of greenish-brown crystal. My response was spontaneous, giving thanks.

Immediately there was another glint, and again I stooped

to find another tiny crystal point, this time black. I became very still. This was very strange. The Earth seemed to be responding to what I said.

I asked to make sure.

There was a flash of light from a tiny dark brown crystal, another double-terminated wand. Before our astonished eyes (or perhaps we were seeing differently) crystals began appearing around us. Each time we expressed gratitude there was a fresh wave.

On hands and knees, we collected a hundred and fifty between us before I said, 'Please stop! We have enough.' It was overwhelming.

But the Earth, it seemed, had not finished. There was yet another wave of crystals. This time black clusters, like small blackberries, circled our feet so that we stood surrounded by little prisms of sparkling light. I had an overpowering sense of Earth communicating with us. There was such a benign feeling in the atmosphere.

Finally, completely overcome and unnerved by what was happening, we fled, unable to handle further developments.

The unimaginable had happened – and this was something I wanted to share with others.

I sought out gatherings where I was likely to be heard, speaking so often about this wonderful experience that I was in danger of becoming a bore to some and a pest to others.

Around this time, my path crossed that of a well-known couple of spiritual teachers and, through this meeting, I finally came to understand the significance of these marvellous crystals. Strangely, I had felt an unaccustomed sense of caution when the man asked for a crystal to keep. I hesitated and said that I would meditate on it.

In my room, curled up on my bed, I closed my eyes and tuned into the crystals. Was it appropriate to give this man a crystal? Before long I felt a communication from the silver voice speaking silently in my head as it had done many times before.

Yes, it was appropriate, providing he carried with him an understanding of the purpose of the crystal. I sat up. It had not occurred to me that there might be a purpose.

'What is it?' I asked. There was a pause, then the voice answered.

- *I am a messenger of Union. I have no knowledge of separation. I hold the deep knowing of the rhythm and cycles and natural pattern in all things. I come from One Truth yet I show you the multi-faceted expression of the Whole.*

In my shamanic way of thinking, this made perfect sense. Stones are no more separate from us than anything else. In a way they are our ancestors, record keepers of everything that has taken place on Earth. Within their ancient structure are mysteries that have yet to be revealed.

I hurried back to the couple.

'Oh perfect!' he exclaimed when I told him. 'We are going to a border town in Ireland where the IRA have been active. When I asked for the crystal, I had it in mind to bury it there. Now I know why.'

Ireland - an island of deep divisions torn apart by conflicting ideologies. The perfect recipient for the tiny crystal.

I had already given many crystals into the safe keeping of shamans and indigenous elders and now, reviewing where the other crystals went, I realized they were going to places of ecological damage or human conflict. Places where people were massacring each other over differing beliefs. Places where people had lost their roots, driven out by the greed of consumerism. This insight and the crystal's message profoundly influenced my viewpoint and activities.

Speaking out in this way, I began to think of myself as one of Earth's caretakers. I came to regard Earth as my most powerful teacher – but I wasn't prepared for the painful truth I received when I fell off a ledge in King's Canyon, a remote and beautiful gorge west of Alice Springs.

Along with a group of fellow healers, I had the privilege of being taken on a special excursion into the gorge by an Aboriginal guide. He knew that we were energy healers and explained things about the landscape and its energies that people rarely hear.

I was filled with a heady excitement not shared by the others. The previous day I had walked through landscape, visiting landmarks I had seen in a dream before leaving England. I had stood, axe in hand, looking across a crescent curve of towering red cliffs that I had drawn in detail – a drawing that was buried beneath clothes at the bottom of my suitcase. I was 'high as a kite' when we entered the gorge, my mind filled with utopian and delusionary dreams of an unfolding life in the Australian wilderness. I saw myself in a lofty role, helping heal 'the Aboriginal Wound' of social injustice.

Almost immediately I received a succinct 'message' that brought me back to earth. Just below us, a short distance away from the track, I spotted a small pool nestling secretly amongst rocks at the foot of an overhanging cliff. I was intrigued by what appeared to be drawings on one of the boulders. Abruptly our guide left the group and headed for the pool. Everyone stopped and waited – all except me.

In my excited state, my sensitivity and sense of appropriateness had become blunted. I left the others and followed him. It is strange how some things we remember with such clarity. I went cautiously, watching where I placed my feet, noticing the wonderful fiery striations that zigzagged the rock surface. The air was filled with a sweet, unfamiliar pungency.

I have no idea what happened next. Suddenly I was hurtling through the air towards the boulders below. Just in time I managed to protect my head with my left hand before landing heavily across a large uneven rock.

I struggled to sit up, aware of horrified voices as the others scrambled down to where I lay. People took turns supporting me against the rock; our guide went for help. The group gave me healing while we waited for the paramedics to arrive - without their input the outcome would have been far more serious. To ease the tension we cracked little jokes, a typical response to situations of this nature.

'Little birds need to be sure their wings are strong enough before they try leaving their nest and flying,' a friend teased me gently. Not for the first time I was being likened to a fallen fledgling.

Fledgling jokes continued to be bandied back and forth until help arrived. 'Gee! Your arm is as crook as an emu's neck!' exclaimed the hearty young paramedic who examined me.

'Is it really bad?' I asked.

'Well... put it like this. Your wrist is like a digestive biscuit that's been trod on.'

She certainly had a way with graphic analogy!

Getting me out of the canyon was very tricky, a slow, laborious job. Members of the group took turns helping the paramedics with the stretcher. Although I was only partially conscious of what was happening I was aware through my haze of the laboured breathing *of those struggling to carry me. They stumbled and slipped across boulders and down the narrow, winding track. Finally we emerged to find The Flying Doctor standing by.*

Flying Doctor! Wow!

I gritted my teeth and endured the pain, as I was loaded into the neat little plane for the short flight to Alice Springs.

The nightmare of examination and admission to hospital passed in a sedated blur, and I was only partially conscious of being transferred to the ward. Soft padding footsteps, the whispering swish of uniforms and the gentle hands that checked my pulse, punctuated my fitful dreams all through that night.

Like the road sign that says STOP, the boulders had given me a message in compellingly simple, direct language. STOP! COME DOWN TO EARTH! The message was simple - to be effective instruments for world change, it is essential to remove rose-coloured spectacles, get feet back on the ground and heads out of the clouds; to fully accept physical incarnation and stop being so cosmic.

Everything is about being in right relationship, whether it is to do with personal relationships or our relationship with our own bodies, the natural world or the rest of humanity. We have only to look at the areas that are continually failing in our own lives to see where our own work has to begin. Only by doing so can we become deeply aware, in the way indigenous people are, of Spirit moving through everything around us and understand the Universal Laws that govern all.

If we are to help humanity survive on this planet, spiritual visionaries need to find the courage to live and operate in this physical reality – and discover joy in life. Maybe our role is that of being foundation blocks and not the pinnacle of the dream.

A GREEK EXPERIENCE – BEING THE CHANGE

'Modern man must descend the spiral of his own absurdity to the lowest point; only then can he look beyond it. It is obviously impossible to get around it, jump over it, or simply avoid it.'
Vaclav Havel
'Every man beareth the whole stamp of the human condition.'
Montaigne
'I learn by going where I have to go.'
Theodore Roethke
'No amount of skilful intervention can replace the essential element of imagination.'
Edward Hopper

Some years ago while cycling in Cyprus, my partner stumbled upon a camp of volunteers working on a green turtle conservation project. In 2009, memories of this camp re-surfaced and triggered in him a thirst for this experience. Over-riding my doubts with his enthusiasm, he persuaded me that six weeks' turtle monitoring on the west coast of the Peloponnese would be a great experience.

I was fearful of the heat, not sure I could cope with the hardship of extremely basic, even primitive camp conditions with people who I knew instinctively would be far younger and fitter than me. But the bush-girl explorer in me, forgotten by the adult world of routine and habit, was calling. I needed the challenge.

Memories surfaced of winter-camping expeditions in the remote parts of the Northern Transvaal. Each morning I had woken frozen, a curled-up ball inside my sleeping bag, trying to protect myself from the harshness of the early morning frost. My body, thoroughly chilled, generated no warmth and there was nowhere inside my downy tube to escape. But thrusting my face out into the open was even worse as I felt the cold air bite into my suddenly exposed cheeks. The early mornings in camp were always a misery until the sun appeared above the acacia scrub, transforming misery into pleasure, in the golden comfort of strengthening sunshine.

Those expeditions were crammed with special moments of real adventure where my explorer-self had full reign. Of lying flat on a hot, grey rock surface that sparkled with flecks of quartz, watching dassie (rock hyrax) scampering in and out of their burrows. The adrenalin rush of horror as I dodged the sticky ambush of webs slung cunningly by large black and yellow spiders between acacia trees; of my first taste of puff-adder stew, and getting a richly deserved stomach-ache from eating raw peanuts that I had stolen from the local peanut farm.

The excitement and adventure of those early camping expeditions stirred in my bones. But it was more than that. It was a chance to deepen the understanding that I had begun exploring in my book, *Quest for Unity*, about the issues of ecological damage and social justice.

That quest altered my perceptions about personal responsibility for the way to live. I could no longer support the paradigm of economic success that governs industrialised nations and which has placed our world in jeopardy. I have always felt that an aspect of my life-journey concerns the physical act of trying to make a difference.

The Greek trip took three months. It was a way of breaking ourselves in to being homeless and car-less for a while. We travelled minimally on public transport, by hitching lifts, staying with friends, in hostels and with host members of a travellers' organisation. I took only what I could fit into one piece of hand luggage. My towel was an ultra-absorbent dishcloth from Lidl. We were challenging ourselves to see how well we could live on an extremely low budget – on average we spent well under £50 a week including rail and sea travel, food and hostel costs. On several occasions we got through the week spending less than £25.

After six weeks of travelling, we arrived at the Peloponnese in Greece. While we orientated ourselves, we stayed in a tiny, old-fashioned hotel in Kyparissia run by a devout and ancient Greek Orthodox couple. She was small, like a plump, black bantam hen, and was every inch the matriarch who ruled her courtyard empire. He was thin, stooped and gently amiable; every time he passed me, he patted me on the shoulder. Her excellent coffee we drank at the courtyard table, nodding our appreciation. An incense burner, used to ward off the flies, sent out wafts of aromatic scent.

African traders - real gentlemen – lived there cheaply in one room, just one rung on the societal ladder above the Roma. They were from several different countries - Nigeria, Congo, and Southern Africa – and spoke English as their common language, as well as passable Greek. They had amazing resolve to educate themselves. Life for them must have been very hard at times, far from their home and loved ones.

The future of a multi-cultural European population was

everywhere to be seen. The Roma gypsies lived on the town's edge in rusted railway carriages sited on abandoned tracks behind the little station. As scrawny as stray cats and dogs, they scavenged what they could from the bins by the side of the road, melting away at the first sign of raised fists and voices. I felt echoes from my South African past, of social exclusion, poverty and hunger, reaching out to grip my heart when I saw the local resentment towards them.

Opposite the station was a direct coach network to Tirana, Romania and Bulgaria, bringing a constant flow of migrant workers hopeful for farming or construction work. The supermarkets had also arrived like hungry predators on the outskirts of town. Within this sleepy coastal town could be seen the growing embryo of a future city - the only brake, the Greek economic crisis.

We became part of an international camp of volunteers helping protect loggerhead turtles from extinction - amazing prehistoric creatures that deserve to make it through to the next century. We lived a semi-feral existence in a tent just behind Kyparissia Bay. Sixty kilometres of magnificent sand dune system backed by garrigue - hummocky aromatic scrubland - and behind that, the last remaining coastal forest crawled up the backing slopes of the Arcadian mountains.

So far the Greeks have managed to leave it alone - not for much longer, I'm afraid. The natural world will vanish from this region unless there is a sudden shift in awareness. Like everywhere else in Europe, Greece seems entrenched in the rapid-growth economic paradigm.

Each morning at dawn, we walked along the beach, our job to scan for the telltale *swim* of turtle tracks, a scalloped-edge trail through the sand that indicated the possibility of a nest. On our knees we dug, fingers sensitive to differing temperature and texture, anticipating the sudden give of loose sand when we located the nest. Once found, it was protected with a metal grid, staked in place with bamboo lengths to thwart predatory dogs and foxes. Nests too close to the sea had to be relocated farther up the beach. It was hot, gritty work and volunteers came straggling back to camp in twos and threes around midday, often too tired to talk.

Daybreak was my favourite part of the day. The early start meant I experienced the cusp between night and day, a magical time when the cold shadow-land of night shifts to the first tentative hints of rose warming the glistening sand. Outside my comfort zone as a volunteer, I became more aware of everything I encountered on these walks.

The sand was beautiful, deep gold, ribboning away into the distance. But close inspection of a handful showed that it was made up of many different colours - pink, black, green, tan, red, grey. Our feet sank deep into its sifting softness, making walking difficult and tiring, but, nearer the tide-line, where wetness had turned the sand red-gold, it was firmer and easier to walk. I liked being at the edge, where the sea washed in and out bringing gifts of tumbling pebbles.

I often joined in a rhythmic dance with the waves, skipping as I tried to keep my feet dry. Walking in that dialogue of motion, I was able to appreciate the many different aspects of the sea – the ranks of white foaming suds at the surf's edge giving way to shades of blue and stretches of purest aquamarine sprinkled with sunlight. A distant mountain, like a reclining woman, rose in blue relief through the heat haze.

Standing in the sea looking for pebbles, I appreciated the infinite variety of stone colours being tumbled in the grinding process of transformation. Farther up the beach the 'sea change' had already taken place, the pebbles ground into fine sand, colours no longer visible - just a beautiful gold in the sun.

Thinking about the camp, I am struck by how the young people, with all their diverse backgrounds and various talents, are like those pebbles at the tide-line. They are on the leading edge, facing the challenges, their differences rubbing up against each other, able to inspire and find creative solutions for camp life. They are like coloured pebbles, combining to create an experience of pure gold.

Teams went out on night patrols from 11pm to 3am to locate nesting turtles. This was a scientific project, so collecting data on the movements and behaviour of turtles was extremely important. During egg laying these strange creatures go into a trance-like state and that's the time to measure and tag them. While others tagged, I lay full length on the sand, watching as eggs the size of ping-pong balls dropped onto a steadily growing pile.

I walked reverently beside the turtles as they made their way back into the sea, listening to their hoarse breathing. There was something very meditative and grounding in the act of walking beside them - the slow pace, the long pauses with stillness descending over me like a cloak, trying to imagine the planetary changes that must have taken place over the aeons of time they had been in existence. Indian mythology says that the survival of the turtle ensures the survival of the world.

In the realm of moonlit stillness, with the sound of the sea's hypnotic movement, affected by the intensely focused effort of the turtle, it was easy to feel inwardly connected with everything in existence.

Being a turtle volunteer was hard work but there was much to laugh about, too. There were frequent moments that were extremely funny - even a few bawdy moments.

Night surveys presented all kinds of hazards. There were snarls of discarded fishing line, rusty tins and jagged driftwood to walk into in the darkness. Then there was always the chance of encountering snakes and scorpions. But not all hazards involved danger.

Night-time is a time of illusions. The dark plays strange tricks on eyes and ears, even after they have adjusted. The first hour of patrol was always the most difficult. It was the darkest time of the night for the moon did not climb above the Arcadian mountain ridge until after midnight.

Ahead lay a deeper patch of darkness on the beach. We stopped and strained our eyes; strained our ears. Listening carefully we thought we could just make out laboured breathing. Yes, we decided, it was a turtle. Our leader motioned us to crouch down and wait. Half an hour later we grew restive. This turtle seemed to be making very slow progress. Perhaps she was sick. We waited a further ten minutes and then the patrol cautiously moved closer. One by one we burst out laughing - we had been watching a large rubber tyre!

Mistakes like that were common, but few could rival what happened the night Ollie took his first patrol.

Ollie, a young New Zealander, was leading the night survey. The group walked along the surf-line scanning the sand for tracks. In the darkness ahead, they heard the clear, unmistakable, heavy breathing of a nesting turtle. Though the shadows were impenetrable, rhythmic scraping sounds carried on the dark night air, indicating she was probably digging.

Ollie motioned the others to stop while he crawled slowly in the direction of the sounds. Inch by inch he wormed his way forward, hardly daring to breath. At last, peering hard, he could just make out the humped back of an exceedingly large turtle. The sounds had now changed to slower, deeper, more even breathing. The turtle must have entered her egg-laying trance.

Ollie risked a quick glimpse with an infrared beam torch. To his surprise and acute embarrassment, two pairs of eyes looked back at him. He had startled a pair of lovers in the throes of their passion.

In Greece I discovered a prodigious amount of consumer plastic littering the beaches: plastic bags, lighters, bottles, fishing line - some still with hooks attached - all posing a real threat to turtles and other marine life. Like many other species, turtles cannot tell the difference between something that is food and something that is not. Vivid *Internet* pictures of the massive floating plastic island stretching between the west coast of America to Japan have had great impact on me. I am haunted by images from Midway Island of the pathetic remains of albatross chicks, their carcasses crammed full of brightly coloured plastic objects regurgitated by their mothers.

Often we passed fishermen patiently casting their lines out to sea in the faint hope of catching a fish. *Kalamera!* I'd call out in greeting, making a show of picking up rubbish as I passed. Usually there were polite nods, maybe a jovial greeting, but sometimes there were surly looks and silence. They knew we were turtle watchers and turtles were mistakenly seen by many fishermen as competitors. They believe the turtles to be responsible for the scarcity of fish -

in fact, fish form only a small part of their diet.

In this impoverished part of Greece we saw the conflict between personal interests and environmental protection. I feel a lot of compassion for the *have-nots* wanting a slice of the 'goody pie' that we, in the rich parts of the world, have benefited from for so long. It is difficult to explain to an outraged fisherman or beach-taverna owner why he should concern himself with turtles nesting on his stretch of the beach, and why we should interfere with him feeding his family.

In camp, we were living the life of the techno-peasants, provided with an opportunity for finding a balance between less money and more time. Here we experienced the developed and emerging nations joining together – and it started with the acquisition of our tent, a donation from a migrant worker in Patras.

R'adar, a young North African migrant, leaned on the rickety counter of the hostel, his welcoming grin wide enough to embrace all of Patras. There was a room for us. Very cheap, he said. He handed each of us two stiff, threadbare towels and a couple of well-worn sheets and pillowcases to cement the deal before we could change our minds. Climbing the dirty stairs, he waved in the direction of the lavatories. 'Very good. Water flush.' Two young Albanian girls with dripping hair appeared on the landing in dressing gowns, looked at us with sulky expressions and disappeared again. We climbed more stairs to a scratched door.

'Your room is very fine,' said R'adar, jiggling the key in the ill-fitting lock. 'You have roof terrace.'

The door opened onto four metal-framed bunk beds, one of which was obviously occupied. A man's jacket hung from a nail beside it and on the floor was a small transistor radio. 'He gone to find job. He not come back tonight.' We looked at each other, grimaced, and agreed rather reluctantly, to stay.

When he had gone, we stood on the crumbling concrete terrace enjoying the last of the afternoon sun and surveyed the grounds, a large plot of prime real estate beside the waterfront. The hostel was a grand old house gone to seed. A battered and dirty building with personality, surrounded by cramped, soulless apartment blocks embedded in tarmac and concrete. Every cat in the district seemed to be in the grounds relaxing, enjoying the sun as we did. There was an air of freedom. Suddenly I felt the seedy squalor was acceptable.

From this point on in our journey we needed a tent. On learning this R'adar, retrieved from a dusty cupboard a tent covered with cobwebs. 'Don't buy! Use this and bring it back when you leave.'

We explained that we would need it for a long time – six weeks. He considered this for a moment. 'You use it for six weeks and then bring it back.'

'But we wont be coming back this way.'

R'adar rubbed his neck as he thought. Finally he said, 'Inshallah! You keep.'

'How much?' we asked.

'No money. Pray for my mother and father.'

Such generosity towards complete strangers I find quite humbling.

At the outset we softened our sleeping with four layers of big bubble wrap that is used for protective packaging (it doesn't pop!). Later, we managed to cadge some thin foam mats for greater comfort.

It was bakingly hot. The only ones enjoying it were snakes and cicadas. The snakes, as in Africa, gravitated to the sun-baked surfaces of tracks and roads, awakening within me childhood memories and ingrained habits of scanning the ground ahead.

The cicadas populated the olive tree shading our tent. Watching them crawling in great numbers along the branches, chirring to each other, was fascinating. They really converse: the chirring varies, changing note and rhythm as new insects enter the sound-stream. If they feel threatened, they shriek, sounding and looking outraged. They have the unpleasant habit of showering those who upset them with excrement. Our tent was encrusted with their outrage by the time we left.

In camp we gained the practical experience of how a community can be built out of nothing by inexperienced but intelligent people. Discovering the value of living without items that we have come to regard as essential was a rich and rewarding part of the healing journey. It was a true rite of passage for them - us too.

Camp life grew as it became more established. After a time with no water, we managed to rig up a standpipe to supply our needs. We arrived in the 21st century when a porcelain loo was positioned in bizarre white splendour atop a septic tank at the edge of the olive grove. In the absence of concrete, the base was sealed with mud to keep the worst smells at bay. At first a cloth screen provided privacy and we hummed loudly to show occupation, but eventually we acquired a wooden shack. Every little innovation was met with universal enthusiasm as if we had received a wonderful gift.

The shower was finally rigged up in our last week with its water tank sitting precariously on the roof of a tumbled down pig-sty. We ran an electric cable down from the taverna and acquired an old electric drill. This was *Third* world meeting *First* world, scavenging anything that looked useful and finding a new use for it. All our seats, shelves and storage units were created out of scraps. Path-edge lighting was provided by bleached white driftwood glowing in the dark.

What I rediscovered for myself was how little we need to survive quite comfortably and happily. How satisfying it is to scavenge and re-create. It brought back those childhood memories of scouring the veldt for rusting wrecks of abandoned cars and carrying away bits of engine to create the adventures that enriched my childhood.

I saw it again more recently in Gambia, while walking past a garage shop in the border village of Kartong. The ground around the garage was littered with discarded bits of metal. Rubbish to British eyes, but in Gambia a new use would be found for everything lying around in the dust.

Our time in camp came to an end earlier than planned. My feet were my downfall, swelling in the heat and they hurt with every footstep. We left our growing international family to work on the front line with the turtle rescue centre near Athens. In spite of being on the edge of civilisation, I found it far more challenging than anything I had experienced in camp. Survival in a city is more difficult, I discovered.

The rescue centre was an heroic venture run on a shoe-string by a small group of dedicated Greeks. There were shortages of everything and no satisfactory way of overcoming them. Here the sense of lack was emphasised by the wealth on display in the marina beside the rescue centre. Multi-million dollar yachts, aloof in their moorings, moved gently on the swell in gleaming lines separated only by boardwalks from the condom-strewn waste ground opposite. I found the contrast upsetting.

Migrant African traders, with trays of unwanted wares and resigned expressions, were there, too, moving amongst the cafe tables trying to earn enough to survive. I admired their determination to escape the hopelessness and helplessness that arises from dependence on aid back home.

The contrast between rich and poor was strongly reminiscent of Sophiatown in South Africa, where Archbishop Tutu had his beginnings. Sophiatown was a sprawling African district, a wonderfully vibrant African presence surrounded by the wealthy white suburbs of Johannesburg. Unwanted and rejected by whites, Sophiatown with all its colour and character was torn down, the people driven out by armed tanks ahead of the bulldozers. They were herded into Soweto outside the city limits, a soulless apartheid solution.

We had a day to orientate ourselves before the next phase of hard work began. Very quickly we saw the need to register the location of hazards for safe walking round the centre after dark. By the path on the way to our sleeping quarters was an open drain filled with foul-smelling water from the turtle tanks. There were objects that could snag, tear, cut and puncture, and we had no wish to experience the medical services of Greece.

Ignoring all my principles about water conservation, I became obsessive about washing my hands as a precautionary measure, not only for my own protection but also for the sick, often badly wounded turtles, some struggling to survive with fishing hooks in their throats.

We had arrived in the middle of a crisis. The saltwater pump had broken down and tanks for thirty turtles had to be filled each day by bucket. Bucketing water into large tanks is gruelling wotk in that heat - but there was no choice. Turtles were swimming in a brown soup of fouled water and some had dreadful injuries – great chunks out of their shells, amputated flippers, deep wounds in their heads from propellers that exposed their brains.

It was a desperate situation.

Turtles are amazing creatures, each with their own

personality. They ranged in sizes from little ones weighing no more than a bag of sugar to giants like Goliath, a newly arrived male turtle waiting to be X-rayed at a private hospital. He weighed about eighty kilos and was well over a metre long. After an unfortunate experience with a turtle named Thomas, the director of the centre knew he would be too big to fit into a lift. Four strong people would be needed to lug him up the three flights of stairs to the X-ray department. Until they could be found, Goliath would have to wait.

Thomas was found lying on a beach and brought to the rescue centre, with sharp tearing barbs hooked into the delicate tissue of his throat. He was the largest loggerhead turtle the centre had seen - weighing 54 kilos and with a 75cm carapace. He needed an X-ray. The problem was that the only place capable of X-raying an animal of his size happened to be in a private clinic near the centre of Athens.

The rescue centre, always struggling on a shoestring, was short-staffed at the time. Only two people could be spared to take him. That posed a big problem. Thomas was very heavy and objected strongly to being handled. Snapping his beak and hissing loudly, he kept everyone at bay. In spite of the obvious difficulties, the centre's director decided the X-ray could not wait. Together with a strapping young trainee vet, he would have to manage somehow.

There was considerable consternation when, on arrival at the clinic, it was discovered that Thomas in his box was too large to fit inside the clinic's narrow lift, and far too heavy to be carried up three flights of stairs.

Thomas had to be removed from his container. But in order to fit him in the lift, he had to be up-tilted on his side, and wedged in place by the director leaning his full weight against him. Thomas took violent exception to being balanced on the edge of his carapace, thrashing his flippers and tail wildly. His blunt head swung back and forth wheezing and hissing in beak-snapping fury.

The young vet pushed the 'UP' button and, even before the door had

BACK TO THE BEGINNING

slid closed, began her race up the three flights of stairs to meet the lift on its arrival. She was almost there when she heard a piercing shriek. Bounding up the last few steps, she found a small Greek matriarch, in the traditional widow's black, leaning against the wall, her hands clutched to her bosom and the director sprawled in the lift. The vet turned at the sounds of further commotion just in time to see the back end of Thomas disappearing through the swing doors of the clinic. He had decided to arrive under his own steam.

The consequence of this fiasco was that the director stipulated that, in future, all large turtles would have to be accompanied by at least four people.

Thomas has now been released back into the wild, none the worse for his adventure.

The new pump came a week later. It is difficult to describe the sense of joy we felt at the arrival of this piece of machinery. It was the most heavenly sight to see tanks full of clean water and the happily splashing turtles.

The chores were grindingly monotonous. Each day there were medication duties, tank cleaning, and the feeding of turtles. The first experience of the day at the rescue centre was the stench of rotting fish. It was nauseating and something that became all too familiar. My overriding sense of disgust at the smell was probably my greatest challenge.

How I loathed it.

Having said that, I would not have missed the experience. It developed my levels of stoicism and challenged me to become a survivor. It provided opportunities to exercise initiative. The experience of building a community from scratch while, at the same time, working to a state of satisfied exhaustion to help save loggerhead turtles from extinction in the Mediterranean, is one I will always remember.

ANCIENT FUTURES - WISDOM OF
THE WAITAHA

*'Behold this and always love it! It is very sacred, and you
must treat it as such.'*
Sioux Nation
'The Land is a mother that never dies.'
Maori
'With all beings and all things we shall be as relatives.'
Sioux Nation

Around my neck hangs a medicine pouch. Inside are
several of the tiny crystals from Spain, a constant reminder
that they are *messengers of unity*. Everything on the planet is
inter-connected. No one knows this better than the hunter-
gatherer societies scattered round the world – the Amazon
and Equatorial rainforest Indians, the Kalahari Bushmen,
the Australian Aborigines. There are others too, like the
Maori and the Waitaha before them, who have not forgotten
the wisdom of their ancestral past.

Shortly after I made the extraordinary discovery of the
axe, Barry Brailsford, a New Zealand storyteller, gave me
two more stones. One was *pounamu* - the Maori name for
nephrite jade - the other a beautiful piece of carved and

polished limestone. Limestone is one of Earth's earliest record keepers - within it we find the fossilised remains of ancient life forms.

By contrast, the piece of *pounamu* was unpolished, yet it had a soft natural sheen. The shape made me think of the arching form of a leaping salmon. Salmon have always fascinated me because of their homing instinct and the way no obstacle, not even a waterfall, deters them from reaching their final destination – the place where they had their beginning. As a result, salmon have a symbolic significance for me. The journey through life is filled with obstacles, many self-made but, like the salmon, I won't give up.

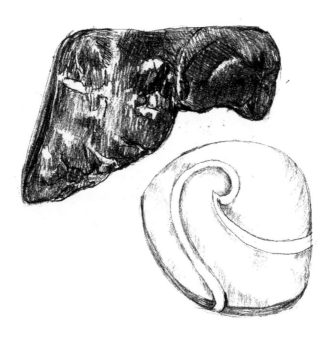

In the years following I did not forget Barry or his fascinating stories. Finally, in 2005, I determined to find out more about an obscure scattering of people Barry had spoken about - the Waitaha. I travelled back to the other side of the world on another quest, this time in New Zealand.

> *'Ruia, Ruia, Ruia nga kakano I Ruia mai i Rangi Atea...*
> *We do this for the children, and their children and all who*
> *call this land home...'*
> *(From 'Song of the old Tides', Barry Brailsford, 2004)*

In the year 2000 I had stumbled across Barry Brailsford, raconteur extraordinaire, playing host to him at my home in Bath. During his visit he kept me and others enthralled with his accounts of the Waitaha Nation. Their origins are older than old. They had settled in New Zealand a thousand years before the warlike Maori arrived. Only a small number of Waitaha, mostly women and children, survived the massacres that accompanied their arrival.

The women were taken as wives, their children adopted into Maori tribes. And there it might have ended as history repeating itself, a culture destroyed by invaders, its existence lost in the mists of time.

What made these Waitaha unique was the fact that they were survivors of a nation made up of different root races. Their forbears had travelled from Europe, the Americas, Asia and Polynesia, in waka - great, double-hulled canoes - navigating the vast distances by following ocean currents and guided by the stars. They settled Aotearoa (New Zealand) and founded a nation based on pacifist principles, following the God of Peace, Rongo Marae Roa. For centuries, they lived without weapons and created trading systems that moved industrial stone the length of the country.

There is a saying amongst the Waitaha, 'If we are not gentle with life, the garden within us dies.' It mirrors their way of life because they are 'Earth honourers'. Their ancestors looked after the land and the water to sustain life, harvesting birds and fish to sustain and increase their numbers, cutting tall trees for their waka in ways that preserved the forest, keeping the environment in balance. Mussel and kelp beds were transplanted to where they would thrive.

Laughter and learning flowed together. In weaving their kites from marsh grasses, children learned how to make windbreaks to shield delicate crops from the prevailing winds. In flying them, they learned to read the nature of the wind. Infants were set beside streams to watch tiny fish shake their gills clear of silt on the stream bed and, from this behaviour, learn whether the water was clean to drink. From stick insects the Waitaha learned whether an area was healthy to grow crops. Where stick insects gathered, the trees were sickly indicating that the soil was no good. They were the forerunners of biodynamic gardening, being guided by the cycles of the moon when planting their crops.

Secretly, descendants of the Waitaha kept the knowledge of their beginnings alive, passing on their history, spiritual beliefs, knowledge and mythology in song. More than sixty generations have kept this history and sacred knowledge safe, hidden in the shadows.

It was not until the early 1990s that the elders of the different Iwi (tribes, clans, families) made a group decision to reveal their history. They found Barry Brailsford (MBE) at Christchurch College of Education. He wrote down, for the first time, the history of their nation in a book titled, 'Song Of The Waitaha'. After generations of being hidden and denied they are now being acknowledged more openly.

In 2005, the conductor of my choir, announced plans for a singing tour to New Zealand. I was tremendously excited for I saw it as an opportunity to search for descendants of the Waitaha and learn what I could at first hand. To my great disappointment, I discovered that Barry would be away on a lecture tour. This was a blow, as I knew my task would be like looking for a needle in a haystack without his help. It was. I met with blank faces everywhere I went.

After the tour ended, I stayed on in New Zealand to continue the search. My first stop was in Nelson where a chance meeting in the market place with a stone carver, Ian Longley, gave me a lead. I had approached him because he reminded me of Barry. It turned out he both knew him and was well acquainted with the history of these elusive people. In addition he had been trained in pounamu carving by a Waitaha elder from the West Coast. That was where I would most likely meet their descendants, he told me.

As we parted, Ian Longley gave me a beautiful flower-jade (a variety of pounamu) pendant. Pounamu, he told me, should never be bought for oneself. Its power lies in it being given as a gift and when received it should be worn close to the skin. It grows in its mana (spiritual power) as it absorbs the oil from the skin. The pendant remained round my neck for the rest of the trip.

Travelling back towards Christchurch, I joined friends from England and together we drove to Castle Hill, an area of spectacular natural formations. In both Maori and Waitaha culture it is a place of power and peaceful pilgrimage, revered by them as the dwelling-place of the Ancestors. In silence, we wandered amongst the cluster of enormous boulders thrusting skywards out of the surrounding landscape like giant fingers. When our paths crossed, we instinctively spoke in whispers, recognizing that we were in a sacred space. The atmosphere of contemplation continued into the evening.

Next day brought a change of mood and pace as we continued our journey by rail to Greymouth. To do this we had to stand by the side of the track and flag down the train as it clattered into sight around the bend. We wound through Arthur's Pass, one of the most scenic routes in all of New Zealand. On every side mountains stood tall; grand though they must be in their summer garb, they towered above us, absolutely magnificent in their snowy winter covering.

Greymouth, by contrast, is a plain place, grey in feeling like its name. But here, at last, my search finally bore fruit. There in a small two-wheeled caravan, parked on a strip of wasteland alongside an industrial building, I found Mick Collins, a descendant and elder of the Waitaha Nation, with a lineage that can be traced back sixty-four generations. He was a truly amazing old man. He lived like a hobo but he was one of the most highly respected jade carvers in New Zealand. He knew how to carve stone without breaking its spirit. Galleries and museums throughout New Zealand commissioned his work.

As we talked, a shiny white car drew up. A natty little sports number. Mick and I watched as its expensively dressed driver picked his way carefully across the waste-ground between piles of rock, hugging a shiny leather briefcase to his neatly suited chest as if he was afraid of banging it on one of the stones. Standing there in the dust, facing Mick in his old jumper and baggy trousers, he tried his best to sell him house and contents insurance. He was very persuasive.

'Everyone has things they value that they would hate to have stolen', he said at last, somewhat desperately. 'You are a rich man!'

I looked at Mick, surprised by that.

Mick started to chuckle. 'I would love to see them try to lift one of these', he said, gesturing to the enormous stone I was sitting on. 'I had to hire a helicopter to lift that one!'

I was astounded! The huge rusty-coloured boulders lying scattered around his caravan were in fact all extremely valuable. Several hundredweight of pounamu, New Zealand jade, just waiting to be used.

'There is more here than I can carve in my lifetime,' Mick chuckled, watching the defeated insurance man walk away.

He showed me a photograph of himself on the side of a mountain supervising the airlifting by helicopter of another boulder weighing more than a ton - part of that now lies in a Rotorua gallery.

Before I left him Mick showed me his tokotoko, his talking stick. On one side the design depicted his European lineage, on the other his Waitaha and Maori ancestry. I have a beautiful book, 'Song of the Old Tides', written by Barry Brailsford, and in it are photographs of the tokotoko.

I felt lucky having made one contact but, before I flew out of South Island, I met another Waitaha descendent. Quite by chance I mentioned my interest in the Waitaha to my hosts at a B & B in the Malvern district on the outskirts of Christchurch. They immediately introduced me to their neighbour, Makere, a Waitaha descendant! Through her, I obtained a rare copy of the book Barry had transcribed, 'Song of the Waitaha' which records their history and philosophy.

The 'Song of the Waitaha' only contained the men's song. Makere had just completed a translation of the women's song in a companion book, 'Whispers of Waitaha'. I became the proud possessor of two absolutely unique books containing the complete spiritual philosophy of an ancient civilization.

As far as I am aware, this is the only example of a philosophy for sustainable living to have ever been passed on orally from the distant past. No other culture has recorded the understanding that the key to continuing existence is closely bound up in knowledge of the elements, life cycles and habits of flora and fauna, regardless of type or kind. The Waitaha understood about preservation and conservation. Everything had to be respected. It all matters.

I had to pay £25 excess baggage because of the weight of the books, but it was worth it.

I returned to New Zealand in 2008, retracing my steps to some of the places that had been meaningful to me on the previous occasion. One of them was the extraordinary landscape of Castle Hill. Perched on top of one of the

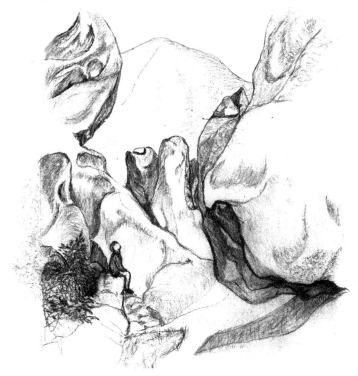

natural rocky giants and surrounded by others, I sensed their power and how they held the story of time in the heart of their crystalline structure.

Sitting amidst all that ancient rock, it was natural think of how the axe had been delivered into my 21st century hands from the slimy ooze of the Severn Estuary. It was such a significant moment.

Do we have something to learn from stone? I believe we do. As a healer, I have been deeply influenced by contact with the mineral world. The geological sense of time is very sobering, very grounding. Rocks have been witness to the miracle of evolving life on Earth over the millennia, and here we are at this critical juncture with everything under threat; life, as we know it, hanging in the balance, probably about to change forever.

Is it possible to create a new world-view built on this understanding? There is evidence that we can. At a *Bioneers' Conference* in California in 2004, author and environmentalist, Paul Hawken, spoke of the phenomenal upsurge of groups involved in social and environmental change, likening it to 'humanity's immune response to resist and heal the damage caused by ideologies'. He referred to a never-ending list of organizations scrolling down a screen behind him, 'What you are seeing here is the beginning of a list of the two million organizations in the world that work towards social and environmental justice - and that's a minimum.'

His concluding words were, 'It's the largest social movement in the history of humankind...by far.' I was electrified by the thought. So many people campaigning for change is an incredibly exciting and hopeful sign.

Here we are teetering on the brink of unprecedented changes, whether we like it or not. We cannot separate ourselves from anything that travels with us through space on this beautiful *spaceship* called Planet Earth. I dare to hope that within the next half decade there will be enough people worldwide ready to step forward and lead the way, inspiring others to change by their example – and to support those who will struggle.

PIVOTAL MOMENTS

'Every single one of us can make a difference.
You can...you can...you can...I can!'
Archbishop Desmond Tutu
'We have not taken the final step of our journey, but the first
step on a longer and even more difficult road.'
Long Walk to Freedom, Nelson Mandela
'If you want to go quickly, go alone
– if you want to go far, go together.'
African proverb

I saw a perfect metaphor for change once demonstrated in a short film. It showed a metal plate covered in spores from a *lycopodium* plant being subjected to sound waves moving up the musical scale from Middle C to D and beyond. At Middle C, the spores arranged themselves into a beautiful, orderly pattern. The pattern was maintained until just before the next pure note. Suddenly, it dissolved in complete chaos only to reform an instant later into a new pattern as the perfectly pitched D was reached.

Before any big change takes place, there is a period of chaos regardless of whether it is in a personal change of direction or on a global scale. It is always messy and bewildering. We lose our balance. Things fall apart, become fragmented.

'I can only move by losing my balance,' I heard someone say in reference to Tai Chi. It holds true in our lives, too. Only when we lose our balance can we move forward. That seems a contradiction, but it isn't. Between every step we take there is a moment when we are out of balance – it is a dynamic moment. Often there is a feeling of discomfort during the transition. For some it is short, for others it can be long. In my case it seemed to take forever.

Nobody chooses change readily. It always means letting go of something. It may be a relationship or a way of life. It may be we have to let go of part or all of the grand narrative of our lives, and that is often very difficult for us. It was certainly true for me. There came a point where my vision of life needed to be clarified and re-defined.

I discovered various aspects of *New Age* thinking and practices no longer served me. But in letting go of them, an enormous part of my life disappeared and everything began to unravel leaving me disorientated and uncertain of direction. I entered a new transition-phase. It was not something that happened suddenly. Bit by bit the shift took place over several years alongside my hands-on healing work. That was also changing its form. Fewer and fewer people were approaching me about ailments. Increasingly, I was drawing people who, like me, were on the brink of shedding their old lives and looking for greater fulfilment.

So how did I arrive here? What were the pivotal moments? It is easier looking back, to pick out significant moments that influenced and steered me to the point where I am now.

Paradoxically, the arrival of the 21st century with its speculation about the future brought back a rush of memories from my South African past. A little bush girl at home in the natural world, yet I was old enough to apprehend the violence and injustice of the repressive Apartheid regime. Now, with an adult's awareness, I can see the disparity between rich and poor widening everywhere.

Van Jones, a human rights lawyer in USA, expressed it well in an interview when he said that we cannot have a whole and healed world while we live in societies that believe we have throwaway resources, throwaway species and throwaway people. Society likes to think it has no responsibility for how they came to be outsiders or for what happens to them later on. Systems like the Apartheid, which capitalized on inequality, are responsible for the increase in the simmering resentment towards wealthy nations. It happens in little incidents.

We waited, thankful for the shade of a large thorn tree, our car third in the line at the border between the Republic of South Africa and Lesotho. Ahead of the cars, a long line of Africans, on foot, queued at the barrier, waiting patiently for their papers to be examined, listening to those ahead of themselves being brow-beaten by a belligerent border control policeman. I listened too, insulted and embarrassed in turn on their behalf. There was no need for the policeman to address them in that manner. He was a bully. He knew they dared not answer back. In Apartheid South Africa, the consequences of that would have been dire for an African!

We sat in our privileged position, feeling sorry for the Africans, many without hats, standing in the full heat of the midday sun. Ahead of us, a fat Afrikaans farmer mopped his brow and complained loudly. As minutes passed his complaints grew louder and louder. Suddenly, he leaned out of the car window and shouted at the border police. I could not follow his rapid Afrikaans but his gestures were plain enough. He was not happy about sitting in a queue waiting for African passes to be processed.

The passport control officer approached the farmer's car, his manner suddenly polite. There was a brief discussion and then, turning, the officer shouted aggressively at the queue of Africans motioning them to step aside. Reluctantly they moved back, but their demeanour remained impassive and they said nothing.

The officer, with an authoritative wave of his hand, motioned all the vehicles with white passengers to move forward into their place. In minutes the passports were stamped and we were across the border. But before our turn came, I had just enough time to register something. It was almost, not quite, hidden behind the carefully masked expressions on brown faces. Lurking in the depths of their glances, I noted the silent message, 'Our time will come.'

There are small indications that show changing attitudes - for example, the emergence of the Fair Trade movement and the increase in ethical business. We are beginning to understand that we cannot separate ourselves any longer from the poor of the world. With increasing focus on global warming, the word interconnectedness, formerly part of *New Age* vocabulary, has now gone mainstream.

In the last twenty years, a bewildering number of messages have issued from spiritual teachers, shamans and psychics from different parts of the world; everything from plainly idiotic, to misguided, to deeply serious. What are we to believe? The doom and gloom merchants shout the end of the world is nigh! The hedonists' answer is why bother to look after anything if it is the end – let's go out with a bang! Religious leaders advocate their own insurance policy of becoming more God-fearing.

Whatever the perspective, all are agreed that big changes are ahead. Adjustments need to be made by everyone to ensure safe passage into a new era. More recently, many scientists have voiced their concerns. They send the same message - more needs to be done, and it needs to be done more quickly!

Until the end of the 90s I had worked alone in my clinic

and with a small group in my healing circle. Then I realized that this was not enough. I needed to join forces with more people of like mind. As if in answer to a prayer, the way unexpectedly opened with an invitation to a healing summit in California. It was the first attempt at a gathering of its kind. A call had been issued to people round the world, inviting them to come and contribute their talents, their expertise and wisdom. Contributions were expected to be offered free of charge. This was to be a gathering of peers and everyone was to pay their own way, regardless of fame.

And they did.

I was introduced to *Creative Health Network* (CHN), an international community of people, mostly women, with a spiritual basis in their life. They were humanitarians, healers and peace-builders, committed to creating a healthier world to leave to future generations.

It was the first time I had come across an organisation such as this, or been surrounded by so many healers. They recognised the impact of our individual and collective choices and saw the need for change in Western cultural thinking. Many members participated in community-focused activities that fostered understanding and acceptance of others. I was enthused by their inclusive vision of a world community. Before leaving California I joined CHN and for six years met every month with other UK members in Glastonbury. Later I set up a branch in my home city of Bath. The position of leader helped me find my voice.

We moved into the new century, many buoyed by optimism for the future, but after 9/11 everything changed. Strength of feeling against Britain's involvement in the war against Iraq impelled me to speak up, and so I became a prolific letter-writer to newspapers up and down the country.

During the same period, I played host to many peace

campaigners and healers, keeping an open house for CHN travellers from round the world. I was happy to be surrounded by people who respected each other's differences. Then, following a small gathering that included two key figures in *Jerusalem Peacemakers*, the UK branch of CHN began changing, away from its global focus towards concentrating on peace and reconciliation in The Middle East. It was valuable work but slowly I felt my own energy withdrawing. I knew it was not my calling. Even so, I struggled with an uneasy conscience until my inner voice intervened.

- There can be no peace between Israelis and Palestinians until they form a new relationship with the land. They need to recognize the Spirit of the Earth and make their peace with Her. Their love for their land must change from one of ownership and acquisition to that of respectful loving partnership. Only then will peace return to the area.

I should have left CHN then but I didn't. I was reluctant to let go of something that had played such a meaningful part in my life, so I continued to support meetings and events. As often happens when there is procrastination, matters were eventually taken out of my hands. It ended in tears, and for a long time I struggled to accept the great sense of loss that followed. But something endured and rose out of the wreckage. I retained my feelings of respect and friendship for the key players in the organization.

I want to tell you about two friends of mine. I hold them here, cushioned in the centre of my heart. Pam died slowly, her life and strength draining away bit by small bit over the years, even as her spirit grew stronger. In the last few years, her passionate devotion to the cause she had made her life's work burned with the fierceness of white heat.

It was at a small international gathering at Pam's house that I first met Ibrahim Abu el-Hawa, a leading light within the organisation Jerusalem Peacemakers. Ibrahim is a small, round elderly man with bad feet and pebble-thick glasses, a stateless Palestinian who never let the lack of a passport prevent him from travelling wherever and whenever he felt the need. Ibrahim has one of the biggest hearts of anyone I have ever met — 'Love on Legs', I call him - but within the organisation he was known as the Ambassador of Goodwill.

Ibrahim adored Pam.

As she became weaker, her lungs, damaged by carbon monoxide poisoning, laboured more and more to give her life-sustaining oxygen. In the end, it became obvious that the only hope for her was a lung transplant. Day after day, week after week, month after month, she lay in bed conducting affairs, keeping in touch, networking tirelessly via phone and email as she waited for a lung to become available. Then came the point when she could no longer see anyone.

Ibrahim desperately wanted to see her but he was told gently this was not possible. 'Pray for her. Send her your thoughts.' But he already did that daily. So, what else could he do for his beloved friend?

Pam had never been to the Holy Land. It had always been her cherished desire to go but her damaged lungs prevented her from making the flight, and this gave Ibrahim an inspired idea. He journeyed to all the special and sacred places of his beloved land and took a small scoop of soil at each site: from beneath the fig tree outside his house on the Mount of Olives, from The Garden of Gethsemane, the children's playground at the Hope Flowers School in Bethlehem, from Ramallah, and the Dead Sea shores — too many places to mention. With the sizeable bag of soil filling most of his suitcase, he obtained his visa and caught a flight to England without telling a soul. He made his way down to Glastonbury by bus and, in the dead of a cold March night, he walked quietly around her house sprinkling the soil until he was satisfied that his beloved friend, Pam, was entirely surrounded, embraced by his country. He had brought the Holy Land to her.

Then he went home. Back to Jerusalem.

I found this out months later when Ibrahim came to stay with me. The lung transplant was a success but Pam's weakened system could not fight the infection that followed and she died in August 2007. As we travelled to Glastoanbury for a celebration of her life, he told me of what he had done, his guttural account broken by bouts of silence, his face buried in his handkerchief as he struggled with his grief. Although few others, to this day, are aware of his clandestine visit, he was rewarded for it in an unusual and comical way.

Ibrahim had made known in advance that his cherished desire was to bury some of Pam's ashes on the slopes of Mount of Olives between the graves of his mother and father. Agreement amongst Pam's friends and family was unanimous, but to everyone's dismay the crematorium could not release the ashes in time for Ibrahim to carry them with him on the journey back to London, where he was staying.

The spirit of Pam's humour was reflected in the solution. Her ashes, contained in a beautiful velvet pouch and cushioned inside a jiffy bag, travelled courtesy of the Royal Mail. They arrived through the letterbox two hours before Ibrahim's flight home.

In death she had made one trip none of the rest of her friends would ever do!

So now, in the Holy Land, her ashes lie buried in the Abu el-Hawa family grave beneath a fig tree on the Mount of Olives. But before he put her there, Ibrahim kept a promise he had often made to Pam. He took her to all the places that she had so wanted to see - Jerusalem, The Garden of Gethsemane, Ramallah, and the Hope Flowers School in Bethlehem...

The final destination was the Dead Sea where Ibrahim took her for a swim, floating on his back with the velvet pouch, resting on the island mound of his rotund belly.

(There is a strange postscript to this story. As I finished writing this and reached to switch on the printer, my phone rang. It was Ibrahim calling from The Mount of Olives. He had just been informed that another close friend of ours - and Pam's - had died suddenly during the night at *The Interfaith Conference* in Cumberland. I found myself speculating whether her death had somehow prompted me to get up at 6.25am and write *Pam's Ashes*. I will never know.)

I met the shaman, Roy Little Sun, during my time with  *Creative Health Network*. He was on a pilgrimage around the world, holding ceremonies and creating medicine wheels for peace. It was while creating one of these wheels, that my footsteps were guided to the burial place of the hand-axe, which in turn led me on the quest to Australia and resulted in the fall in Kings Canyon.

Recovering from that accident gave me plenty of time to review how idealistic thinking had clouded my vision. My conviction deepened that our sense of peace, our health and fulfilment depends on being in balance with other living systems and understanding that we are part of everything, not separate.

The health of the planet is linked to our own. Having healed and healthy people depends on having a healed and healthy planet.

It no longer felt appropriate to work solely with the power of thought and prayer in a meditative space amongst like-minded people. If I really wanted to advocate change, I needed to reconnect with aspects of my life I had left behind years before. I would have to become better informed about areas I had been shunning, convinced they would harm me spiritually - the socio-political and economic areas, the material world of consumerism, the news - and start applying all the principles, insights and spiritual tools I had learned over twenty-five years. Like many others, I believed that not just individuals but all of humanity, indeed Earth herself, is on the brink of an evolutionary leap.

It was at a *Great Rethinking Conference* in Oxford that I first heard the term *sacred activism*, used by the radical spiritual orator, Andrew Harvey. He declared, '...Mystics must ground themselves in real active service. And those who are active in the world have to go back to a deep inner practice that will feed them the wisdom, the power, the strength and the energy that they will need.'

He spoke passionately of the need for all of us to be fuelled by 'a vision of the Absolute and a passion for justice. But now it must happen on a huge scale'.

His final words brought everyone to their feet.

'If you bring together the illumination of the Divine Identity with the passion of the Divine Love, and the passion for the divine love for justice, then what you have is a human being that is simultaneously rooted in deep peace and capable of enormous passion, simultaneously rooted in the dark and the light, simultaneously both male and female, simultaneously in heaven and on earth. And therefore you become someone who can be a fearless light warrior, a fearless lover and a fearless, radioactive nuisance to all those in power.'

His speech was brilliant! He was right. Wonderful things can happen when human will is aligned with The Divine. Andrew Harvey's speech was a tremendous validation of my new way of thinking. I had come a long way over the years.

For the next five years I was restless, unable to find a

satisfactory expression for the sense of urgency I felt. It seemed like my footsteps had lost their direction yet again. Then I stumbled upon a facilitator training for a symposium called *Awaken the Dreamer; Change the Dream,* and pure instinct prompted me to apply. I had no idea what I had signed up for until the introductory information arrived. Instantly, I recognized we shared the same vision. It provided another chance to link with an international network similar to CHN, which incorporated spiritual insight and fulfilment into every aspect of life, including the areas I had previously shunned. The better gender balance gave the movement the necessary grounding for effective change.

The symposium has remarkable origins. It was conceived by a group of Californians following a visit to pristine tropical rainforest in Ecuador. They went prompted by messages they had been receiving in dreams and meditation - messages sent telepathically by shamans of the *Achuar* people in the Amazon region of Ecuador. In the late 80s, the elders of the tribe had recognised the need to make contact with the outside world as a way of protecting their lands from oil industries that were already destroying neighbouring environments.

The history of the *Achuar* - and that of other tribes in the region – is an interesting one. At some point in their history, they had willingly undergone major changes of life-style as a means to survival. They were originally a war-like people. Then something occurred which led them to make the decision to join forces with other tribes. They made peace and learned to co-operate for the good – and the survival - of all.

The *Achuar* told their American visitors that in order to protect the Earth for future generations it would be necessary for the industrialised nations of the world to start making big changes. In response, Bill and Lynn Twist set to work to create the symposium *Awaken the Dreamer; Change the Dream*. The goal was to establish a change of focus away from consumerism and rapid economic growth, towards equity, sustainability and spiritual fulfilment. The result was a remarkable tool for inspirational change.

Suddenly, I had access to visual material and constantly updated information at my fingertips – and a global network of committed friends. It was all very exciting. Not surprisingly, my dreams began to reflect issues highlighted in the symposium.

I dreamed last night of feathers, Blue Jay feathers floating past the window. American Blue Jay! So beautiful. Acquisitive thoughts replace more elevated ones - I must have them! I rush through the door, hearing screeching cries of distress but the desire for those beautiful blue feathers overrides everything.

I collect a handful of feathers before the insistent voice of conscience grabs my attention, commenting on my avarice and indifference. For a moment I am conscience-stricken, and, storing the feathers safely, I go searching for the jay.

The bird is lying amongst bushes, severely mangled. Deep head wounds ooze blood. Most of its feathers are gone. I know it will not survive, so I set it down in the bushes again and carry on collecting feathers. The bird is quickly forgotten. Back indoors, however, my conscience is not happy with my choice. I could have done something for the bird; at least had the compassion to dispatch it quickly. I know my choice and values have been selfish.

I wake, understanding the dream is a metaphor for our time. It is another story about stuff. (*Story of Stuff* is a short film created by Annie Leonard, a campaigner against injustice in consumerism. Consumer desire for something cheap overrides awareness and compassion for those being damaged in the process.)

All the signs indicate that our future lies not in trying to preserve the present way of life but in adopting elements of a different philosophy - one that is already upheld by hunter-gatherers around the world; those in the Amazon rainforest and in New Guinea, the Eskimos and the Bush-men of Botswana and the Kalahari. 'We have to look back at the future we left behind,' Jeremy Narby, the anthropologist, commented. 'Now more than ever we need to heed the lessons from our past – take a step back before we move forward.'

In common with the Waitaha, the worldview of our present day hunter-gatherers is based on reverence and respect for all, demonstrating balance and conservation by taking only what is needed. They feel connection with and joy in the natural world. The greatest potential for a successful future is if both our culture and theirs start talking, listening to each other and sharing knowledge. Out of dialogues such as these, something new can emerge for the future.

Perhaps, I am a dreamer. But as the song says, I am not the only one.

EPILOGUE:
AT THE TURNING OF THE TIDE

'The day will come when, after harnessing the winds, the tides and gravitation, we shall harness for God the energies of Love. And on that day, for the second time in the history of the world, man will have discovered fire.'
Teilhard de Chardin
'Man is asked to make of himself what he is supposed to become to fulfil his destiny.'
Paul Tillich
'We cannot escape fear. We can only transform it into a companion that accompanies us on all our exciting adventures...'
Susan Jeffers

I am back to the beginning, finishing where I started. There is so much that I cannot and may never be able to express about my healing work, and I am aware that much has been left out. But this was never intended to be a healing manual. My work is too intuitive.

On my altar are the objects significant to my story. The snakeskin lies in the front to represent the skins I have shed. On either side are placed the significant stones that have come into my keeping; gifts of the Earth that have taught me so much. Each has contributed insight that increased my understanding and broadened my healing ability. The small crystals from Spain, my first stone messengers, *spoke* to me of the interconnection of everything on the planet; how all of life is governed by rhythms, cycles and patterns. They *spoke* of the many facets of Truth reminding me of the differing perspectives I will encounter. It was their appearance that demonstrated our beautiful Earth is alive and will communicate with us if we are open.

Beside the crystals lies the stone spiral reminding me of the *Divine Principle*, the creative life force that expresses itself in the spiralling dance of life. It exists in everything and is the glue that connects us all.

On the far side of the table is the *pounamu* shaped like a leaping salmon, with its companion stone, the carved piece of limestone. They represent the wisdom of the Waitaha, a

nation shaped long ago out of different cultures and races and living in peaceful co-existence with nature. Their Earth-honouring worldview, and that of other indigenous, hunter-gatherer societies, goes back thousands of years, back to the time my Neolithic axe was created.

The hand-axe has been given pride of place on the table along with its finger of stone. Nothing in my journey as a pilgrim healer has affected me so deeply as finding the hand-axe.

This ancient tool is a silent reminder, an embodiment of knowledge and skills from the distant past. Holding it, I reflect on all the memories held in its ancient crystalline structure from the time it was fashioned. It must have taken months, maybe years, to make and much attention was given to its shape. The contours are beautiful, opposites held in balance. Viewed from above, one end is wide, rounded in a pleasing curve, the other end tapers to a blunt point. In profile, the bowed polished surface has been honed at the widest end into a sharply incisive cutting edge - diverse elements embodying my symbol of unity. When differences are brought together, something new and exciting is possible.

The candle flame flickers in a sudden draught. Raindrops drum against the window. As a child in Africa an imminent storm used to fill me with squirms of excitement. I loved the drama, the silent flicker of lightning, like a snake's tongue tasting the parched the earth, darting out from behind the clouds, the first barely heard hint of thunder beyond the horizon; the increasing gusts of freshening air. Then chaos erupting as the storm launches itself, a fury of battering rain and strobe lightning. It mattered not which African country I was in – South, East or West – the same drama played itself out.

Watching the rain today through the double-glazed window, I wonder if our moods are creating our weather. All the depression, the despondency about redundancies and home seizures being played out in the weather. Is the sky weeping the tears of millions?

Gloomy sentiments to match the times, it would seem. The media is focused on a possible worldwide economic slump. Climate change is making itself felt. There is a general air of global chaos, with large regions affected by food and water shortages or altered by violent weather patterns. There is much to feel alarmed about. My concern is for those struggling for survival in disaster-hit areas, as well as those in the developed nations finding the carpet of their familiar world pulled from under their feet, as jobs are cut, homes repossessed.

Yet, despite this, there are reasons for hope.

Change comes at the tipping point of chaos. We are waking up to find the money-utopia of the industrialized age is turning into a nightmare. Increasing numbers of people in developed countries realize that the economically driven technological age and consumerism hasn't brought the peace of mind, or the happiness and fulfilment that was promised. They feel the hunger of lost connection with nature.

Many are recognizing the need for change and are seeking reconnection by trying to understand worldviews other than their own, in particular those of Earth-honouring people. To me this is welcome, a healthy evolution of much needed wisdom and responsible discernment. This is our opportunity to extricate ourselves and reset the course for a different future that is sustainable, equable and fulfilling. But setting a new course is also scary.

A fresh spattering of raindrops hits the window. Water has always been a sign of renewal for me – and also, a sign of emotional release and healing. Pent-up emotions are discharged in moments of catharsis, the water of our tears dissolving and releasing outgrown habits and beliefs. We are left spent and empty in the space of acceptance before being filled with renewed hope, strength and energy to face a future with all its unknowables.

This is water's strength - the act of cleansing and renewal.

Handling emotional intensity has always been my greatest challenge and, not surprisingly, water has played a dominant role as a result. One more horizontal scar on my stomach and I will be able to play *noughts-and-crosses*. Two of these scars are the result of a horrific accident that happened, as a teenager, while surf-boarding on Tarqua Island (as it was known then) off the Nigerian Coast.

It was not until the millennium, the year when I went to South Molle, one of the Windward Islands off the coast of Australia, that my fear of water began to ease, allowing me to re-connect with the wonder and appreciation I had experienced as a child.

Sunset, South Molle - I stand calf-deep in water in a tranquil, meditative state, musing with wonder at how the waters lapping round my legs will eventually find their way round the world until they wash

against the shores of Britain. In the quiet space of time it takes for the sun to slip over the horizon, I watch drops of sea water, infused with gold-orange light, hang suspended from my finger tips before they drop back once more into the sea.

Night's shadows are creeping out of the forested slopes as I splash to shore. In the half-light, I run my fingers through coral fragments that litter the beach, glistening luminous white pieces of filigree from the Great Barrier Reef, awakening memories of Inhaca, the magical island of my childhood dreams.

Inhaca, a small, isolated dot in the Indian Ocean, lies a few miles off the coast of Mozambique and, in common with South Molle, a coral reef runs the length of its eastward shore. Every couple of years my father took students to the marine biology station that he had been given permission to build there by the Mozambique government – and sometimes the family went, too.

I stand in the water at low tide gazing into the exotic world of coral pools where beautiful, glossy leopard-spotted cowries inch across the bottom; where luminous blue-grey starfish studded with brilliant orange spots finger the jagged coral sides with a thousand tiny suckers and striped dragon fish raise their back spines in warning; where tiny electric blue fish and guppies flit nervously from one piece of cover to another; where large grey crabs edge sideways between colourful groups of sea anemones, clack vermilion-red claws in warning when I step too close.. I soak it in, drawing it deep within, absorbing it into my bones. The enchantment surfaces now from memory's depths, dances alive as I write about it.

What do I think now about water? Is it my enemy or my friend? Without a doubt it is a powerful friend. Water has been an important teacher, in making me confront my greatest challenge – fear. The mystic Sir George Trevelyan once said. 'We are all droplets in the ocean of God.' His words touched my depths, anchored themselves in my cellular knowing. I have loved that image ever since.

It was in Greece that I found the confidence to explore outside my comfort zone in water. I was able to take my feet off the bottom and, for the first time in years, enjoy the freedom of swimming in the open sea. No longer did I fear that *Jaws* might be lurking beneath me! Or that I wouldn't be able to reach the shore. It had taken a lot of determination to break through my fear and resistance.

Some patterns are particularly hard to break. Evidence of this can be seen in society's resistance to altering consumer habits. It is difficult to change what we have become used to – but we are all being challenged to step outside our comfort zones as we face the necessity of adjusting to changes in life-style.

So here I am along with everyone else. My footsteps have led me to the brink of an unknown future. I feel both excited and fearful, wondering whether I am equipped to handle the coming challenges. Looking down, I can see that my footprints are no longer alone. They have been joined by countless others all heading in the same direction. Suddenly I feel that I <u>am</u> equipped - this fills me with excitement.

In Greece, I had stood in the surf and watched the pebbles tumbled back and forth by the tide. This edge, where the tide turns, is where the greatest activity and chaos takes place. I believe that we are at this turning point – here change can really happen.

Will we take the opportunities offered? I think we will.

I awoke this morning from a potent dream. I stood on the threshold of myself looking up at a tall spear and a pole planted in the earth. They were in alignment so that only one shadow was cast. A distant figure - an aboriginal figure - stood on the horizon, watching me. I raised my arm in the air, a salute of readiness and greeting - up high like the spear before me. In acknowledgement, the aboriginal figure echoed my gesture and started walking towards me.

He steps across the threshold. The aboriginal self come home.

Spaceship Earth

If they could see Earth, football-size,
Revolving in space before their eyes,
They would stop,
And stare,
And gasp at the beauty.
Would wonder at deep blue oceans
Where icecaps floated,
And whales spouted.
Where flying fish skimmed in silver squadrons
Over foam flecked waves.
And hearts softening, would swell with love,
Find peace in the beauty of rolling plains and
golden sands.
Be transported by lush jungles, splashy with colour,
And awed by the splendour of mountains
Thrusting grey fingers of rock towards their gazing
eyes.
They would wonder at tiny creatures
Moving across the surface,
Amazed at their variety,
Awed by their complexity,
And say,
'Miraculous! Unique!
- The most precious thing in existence.
Preserve it! Protect it! Cherish it!
Defend it! Nothing should endanger it.'
This, they would say if...

If Earth was just football-size
Turning silently in space before their eyes.

QUEST for UNITY
With Silver Voice and The Trickster

This is a time of extraordinary change. Mind-expanding, life-changing things are happening to ordinary people

Quest for Unity is a fast-paced and intriguing account of the mysterious discovery of an ancient stone axe and the quest it initiated. The story follows the author's adventures with all the twists and turns that Coyote, the Trickster, presents along the way, teaching us never to assume anything...

'Quest for Unity is lucidly and fascinatingly told, a fine recounting of the kind of thing that happens when you follow your calling – and it's full of multivits for the soul.' Palden Jenkins (*Healing the Hurts of Nations* and *Only Planet of Choice*)

Kirsten Bolwig comes from a background of science, open spirituality and human rights activism. Describing herself as a spiritual activist, the focus of her spirituality expresses itself in the understanding that today it is no longer appropriate to limit spirituality to contemplation and meditation alone. It needs to be synonymous with action and with the application of spiritual insights, understandings and principles in all areas of life.

She has a strong interest in bringing people of Western culture together with those of ancient traditions as the way to foster deeper spiritual, ecological and collective awareness, seeing this as key to creating a more harmonious future of peace and balance.

Working in Bath, England, as a transformational healer, she views everything in all its diversity as an integral part of the Whole.

kirsten@kirstenbolwig.com